OECD ECONOMIC SURVEYS

1998-1999

AUSTRIA

ORGANISATION FOR ECONOMIC CO-OPERATION AND DEVELOPMENT

ORGANISATION FOR ECONOMIC CO-OPERATION AND DEVELOPMENT

Pursuant to Article 1 of the Convention signed in Paris on 14th December 1960, and which came into force on 30th September 1961, the Organisation for Economic Co-operation and Development (OECD) shall promote policies designed:

- to achieve the highest sustainable economic growth and employment and a rising standard of living in Member countries, while maintaining financial stability, and thus to contribute to the development of the world economy;
- to contribute to sound economic expansion in Member as well as non-member countries in the process of economic development; and
- to contribute to the expansion of world trade on a multilateral, non-discriminatory basis in accordance with international obligations.

The original Member countries of the OECD are Austria, Belgium, Canada, Denmark, France, Germany, Greece, Iceland, Ireland, Italy, Luxembourg, the Netherlands, Norway, Portugal, Spain, Sweden, Switzerland, Turkey, the United Kingdom and the United States. The following countries became Members subsequently through accession at the dates indicated hereafter: Japan (28th April 1964), Finland (28th January 1969), Australia (7th June 1971), New Zealand (29th May 1973), Mexico (18th May 1994), the Czech Republic (21st December 1995), Hungary (7th May 1996), Poland (22nd November 1996) and Korea (12th December 1996). The Commission of the European Communities takes part in the work of the OECD (Article 13 of the OECD Convention).

Publié également en français.

Table of contents

● ● ● ● ●

Boxes

Tables

Figures

BASIC STATISTICS OF AUSTRIA

THE LAND

Area, (1 000 sq. km)	84	Major cities, 1991 census	
Agricultural area (1 000 sq. km), 1996	34	(thousand of inhabitants)	
Exploited forest area (1 000 sq. km), 1996	33	Vienna	1 540
		Graz	238
		Linz	203
		Salzburg	144
		Innsbruck	118

THE PEOPLE

Population, 1997 thousands	8 072	Net migration, 1997, thousands	3
Number of inhabitants per sq. km	96	Total employment,[1] monthly average 1997,	3 056
Net natural increase, 1997 thousands	5	thousands	
Net natural increase per 1 000 inhabitants, 1997	0.6	of which: Primary sector	26
		Secondary sector	967
		Tertiary sector	2 063

PRODUCTION

Gross domestic product in 1997 (Sch billion)	2 514	Industrial origin of GDP at market prices,	
GDP per head, US$, in 1997	25 532	1997 (per cent)	
Gross fixed capital formation in 1997	554	Agriculture	1
Per cent of GDP	22	Industry	22
Per head US$	5 627	Construction	8
		Other	69

THE GOVERNMENT

Per cent of GDP in 1997		Composition of Federal Parliament:	Seats
Public consumption	18.4	Socialist Party	71
General government current revenue	48.1	Austrian People's Party	53
Federal government debt, end 1997	57.6	Freedom Union	40
		Liberal Forum	10
		Greens	9
		Last general election: December 1995	

FOREIGN TRADE

Exports of goods and services, as a per cent of GDP, 1997	42.3	Imports of goods and services as a per cent of GDP, 1997	42.9
Main exports in 1997 (per cent of merchandise exports):		Main imports in 1997 (per cent of merchandise imports):	
Food, beverages, tobacco	4.3	Food, beverages, tobacco	5.8
Raw materials and energy	4.7	Raw materials and energy	9.3
Semi-finished goods	15.2	Semi-finished goods	13.6
Finished goods	75.8	Finished goods	71.3
of which: Consumer goods	49.5	of which: Consumer goods	48.0

THE CURRENCY

Monetary unit: Schilling		Currency units per US$, average of daily figures:	
Currency units per euro on 1st january 1999	13.7603	Year 1997	12.20
		February 1999	12.28

1. Wage and salary earners.
Note: An international comparison of certain basic statistics is given in an Annex table.

This Survey is based on the Secretariat's study prepared for the annual review of Austria by the Economic and Development Review Committee on 23 March 1999.

•

After revisions in the light of discussions during the review, final approval of the Survey for publication was given by the Committee on 21 April 1999.

•

The previous Survey of Austria was issued in April 1998.

Assessment and recommendations

*Overview of
current policy
issues*
At the time of the previous review in February 1998, economic prospects were favourable, with activity picking up and Austria about to meet the macroeconomic criteria for EMU entry. In the event, growth proved even stronger than expected in 1998, despite the Asian crisis and the turmoil on world financial markets, and Austria became a founding member of the Economic and Monetary Union on 1 January 1999. EMU membership has replaced the Deutschemark link with a new monetary policy framework based on euro-area wide monetary conditions, while fiscal policy is now constrained by the Stability and Growth Pact and the associated national stability programmes. At the same time, the ambit of European policy co-ordination has widened to include co-ordination in the area of employment promotion, with the issuance of guidelines for the development of National Action Programmes for the promotion of employment. These will contain verifiable targets to be reviewed on a peer group basis. Against the background of increasing EU integration but slowing world demand, the *Survey* begins with a review of short-term prospects (Chapter I). It then reviews the ongoing fiscal consolidation programme (Chapter II), which raises important issues of public sector efficiency, control over social programmes and containment of public pension commitments. Fulfilling the government's commitment to a tax reform in 2000 with a net reduction in the tax burden constitutes a special challenge in this context. Chapter III discusses the progress made towards more flexible labour and product markets, building on the policy recommendations made for Austria under the OECD *Jobs Strategy* in the 1997 OECD *Economic Survey of Austria*. An important recommendation of the *Jobs Strategy* is the need to

support an entrepreneurial climate, and the policy issues associated with this objective are reviewed in Chapter IV.

Growth has slowed but the deceleration should be limited

GDP expanded by some 3¹/₄ per cent in 1998, driven by strong domestic demand and buoyant exports. However, activity slowed markedly in the second half of the year and business expectations have deteriorated to levels last seen at the start of 1995. GDP growth is projected to slow in 1999 to around 2¹/₄ per cent, as exports slow and investment adjusts to both lower export demand and renewed softness in the construction sector. Continued growth of domestic demand should, however, limit the extent of the slowdown. Consumer sentiment has remained resilient, supported by rising household real disposable incomes, based on low inflation, a stable fiscal burden and a pick-up in employment. Employment growth is now slowing somewhat, but consumer demand is projected to grow by some 2 per cent, which should in turn support capital spending by domestically-oriented sectors. Despite the projected slowdown, the macroeconomic fundamentals are sound, with moderate wage developments and favourable price and productivity trends supported by a macroeconomic policy conducive to growth. As a result, the slowdown is projected to be only temporary and GDP growth is projected to recover in 2000 to around 2¹/₂ per cent, underpinned by a gradual recovery in world trade.

Downside risks are significant, but underlying conditions are sound

The turbulence in world financial markets had only a limited direct impact on the Austrian economy, despite the relatively large bank exposure to Russia and other emerging market economies, but the more volatile international environment means that the projection is associated with greater uncertainty than usual. Moreover, the downside risks of the global financial crisis in terms of its influence on world trade and investment activity are accentuated by the interdependence of the economy with Germany, where business confidence has recently weakened markedly. Nevertheless, though significant, the downside risks need to be kept in perspective. EMU accession has been part of an ongoing process of European integration which continues to benefit Austria and makes for rather good fundamentals. In the event of any negative shock encompassing the euro area, monetary policy could be expected to adjust and fiscal stabilisers at the national level would be allowed to work, at least in the short run.

Monetary policy remains supportive of growth

Monetary conditions were supportive of growth during 1998 and remain so. Policy rates were only changed once when, in a co-ordinated action with other central banks of the euro area, the repurchase rate was lowered by 20 basis points in December to 3 per cent. During the year, core countries with the lowest policy rates – which included Austria – maintained a stable stance, permitting convergence by other euro zone countries to occur at this lower level. Long rates, on the other hand, have declined substantially, in line with those in Germany, falling to 3.6 per cent in the wake of a general flight to quality since October. With inflation low and decelerating, inflation expectations may also have been adjusted downwards, but real interest rates, however measured, are still low relative to their levels over the last two decades. While the yield curve flattened in the course of 1998, this was due to a marked decline in long-term rates and does not indicate a tightening of monetary stance. Despite some major world exchange rate realignments, the effective exchange rate has been broadly stable, the combination of falling interest rates and the absence of any pressure on the exchange rate reflecting the credibility of Austrian monetary policy. At the same time, with unit labour costs also steady, the real exchange rate has continued its downward trend of recent years, with benefits for Austrian competitiveness. Responsibility for monetary policy formally passed to the ECB on 1 January 1999, which will determine monetary policy on the basis of conditions in the whole euro area. With the Austrian cycle now in quite close phase with the EMU core this is not expected to cause problems from a conjunctural point of view. Indeed, with actual and expected inflation low in the euro area, monetary conditions are assumed to remain favourable throughout 1999 and 2000, acting to limit the expected slowdown.

Following the successful fiscal consolidation, the pace of future deficit reduction is quite slow...

Fiscal consolidation was successful in bringing down the general government deficit as a share of GDP from 5 per cent in 1995 (with a tendency to increase) to 1.9 per cent in 1997. This has been a notable achievement, but the pace of consolidation has since slowed significantly. Despite unexpectedly rapid growth in 1998, expenditures also came in above budget, so that the deficit is likely to have risen to about 2.2 per cent of GDP. In accordance with the Stability and Growth Pact, the government plans a further reduction to 2 per cent of GDP in 1999 and to 1.7 per cent in 2000, the objective presented in the 1998 Stability Programme being to reduce the deficit to 1.4 per cent of GDP in 2002. By that time, the debt/GDP ratio, aided by further privatisation and restructuring of the public sector, should have declined from 63 per cent in 1998 to the Maastricht reference value of 60 per cent. The budget deficit target will ensure adherence to the 3 per cent limit under normal business cycle conditions. However, OECD calculations indicate that a budget deficit of 2 per cent – the OECD baseline estimate for 1999 and 2000 – represents the minimum requirement to avoid breaching the ceiling in the case of a normal cyclical downturn. If the economy were to suffer from a series of more adverse shocks discretionary action might be needed to keep the deficit under 3 per cent of GDP, involving at worst damaging pro-cyclical fiscal action. The consolidation plan should thus be more ambitious with respect to the pace of consolidation and to the final budget target.

... and growing pressure from social programmes needs to be contained...

Moreover, the gradual nature of the medium-term fiscal consolidation process has to be seen against the background of ongoing public pressure for higher social spending, which could threaten tax and deficit objectives in the years ahead. Although some programmes were curtailed as part of the 1996/1997 fiscal consolidation package, social expenditures were above budget in 1998 and new social programmes (including the family benefit reform and some labour-market expenditures) have been agreed in the past year which will add Sch 15 billion (½ per cent of GDP) to expenditures and foregone revenues in 2000. While social objectives need to be taken as given in the formulation of economic policy, the public expenditure process, in this case, did not evaluate objectives sufficiently closely in terms of other opportunities foregone *e.g.* tax reform. More generally, past *Surveys* have identified a number of costly entitlement programmes with a regressive content (*e.g.* housing subsidies) which would benefit from a clearer focus. And the constitutional requirement that the tax treatment of children should be equalised between different family types could probably have been satisfied at a significantly lower cost than the actual Sch 12 billion produced by the political negotiation process. This decision severely limits the scope for tax reform and/or more ambitious fiscal consolidation and calls for the development of a process which allows a proper evaluation of choices and trade-offs at the decision-making stage of the budget process.

... but the public administration is becoming more cost-efficient

Increasing pressures from entitlement programmes should be viewed against the significant progress which has been made towards improving both the functioning and the structure of the public administration and the co-ordination between federal government and the Länder, which should help to enhance budget discipline and reduce the former tendency (evident in the 1993-95 period) for expenditures to deviate from plan:

- Performance indicators and benchmarking have been developed for a number of public sector activities and are being expanded. The civil service is being reformed and tenure has been restricted.
- Commercial entities have been shifted into the enterprise sector at all levels of government and they are now required to produce evidence of proper management.
- The implied costs of programme decisions for other levels of government now need to be assessed for every legislative measure and, in the absence of agreement, the initiating level must bear the cost.
- The federal government, states and communes have agreed a domestic complement to the Stability and Growth Pact with binding allocations of the Maastricht deficit limit to the different levels of government.

With respect to the first two areas of reform, it should be noted that the criteria for promotions still remains restricted in favour of insiders, while the requirement of proper management of commercial entities has proved difficult to monitor in many countries in the absence of rigorous market testing, which needs to be expanded by market opening. As for the last two initiatives, these should help to contain some of the pressures for social spending noted above, but the effects will be limited so long as the lower levels of government rely mainly on revenue sharing with the federal government. This will be re-negotiated in 2000, and the new agreement will need to be flanked by greater own revenues for lower levels of government.

Tax reform needs to focus on lowering effective rates

After reviewing the options presented by the Tax Reform Commission in November 1998, the government has decided that, apart from increased family allowances, a further Sch 18 billion should be given back to tax payers. The officially-preferred outline thus now embraces net tax reductions of Sch 30 billion (around 1 per cent of GDP). Additional energy taxes will not be introduced and communal taxes and federal support for residential construction accruing to the states will also not be touched. Beyond that, many key questions remain outstanding, including how the "net tax relief" of Sch 30 billion is to be financed. The 1998 *Survey* noted that although the tax system did not appear to be the source of severe distortions, social security and labour taxes were high and the taxation of capital income relatively low, so that pressures had emerged for a rebalancing. It also noted that the room for manœuvre was limited, so that reducing the overall taxation burden on labour would need to involve a more determined attack on spending programmes with a regressive content. This should remain a priority in deciding the financing. The Tax Reform Commission presented a series of proposals to the government covering the reduction of special income tax deductions, reforms of the inheritance and gift taxation, the unification of taxation across types of capital income and greater reliance on user charges. Each of these proposals goes in the direction of greater tax neutrality recommended by the 1998 *Survey* and should be implemented by the government.

Approved pension reform measures need to be implemented

The Commission also proposed changes to the taxation of private pensions, placing all schemes on the same basis and taxing only pension income. A government-added annual bonus would be used to make contributions and capital income tax exempt and a subsidised private pension scheme would be introduced. These proposals need to be seriously considered, but in the context of the wider question of pension provision. Although pension reforms over the last two years constitute a breakthrough in a number of areas, the legislated amendments will generate only modest savings and do not resolve the fiscal pressures which an ageing population will create. An important aspect of the reform was the decision to correct the annual pension adjustment formula for the change in life expectancy, but its introduction, originally set for 1998, was deferred in order to avoid a small rise in pensions. Action is needed in this area and a further deferral should be avoided. Where reforms have become operational, they have been partial and have, as expected, produced tensions: tightening conditions for early retirement due to old age has reduced the flow of early retirees only marginally because it has led to a greater take-up of invalidity pensions. This scheme needs to be tightened.

The government has adopted a broad-based employment strategy, further expanded in a National Action Programme

The government's policy framework for structural reform to promote employment and growth has evolved in the course of 1998, with the agreement between the government and the social partners on the National Action Plan for Employment (NAP). The remit of the action plan is based on a broad set of recommendations regarding, *inter alia*, the development of skills, the diffusion of technology, and support for an entrepreneurial climate, while recognising the essential inter-relationship between these elements if employment and economic performance is to be raised on a sustainable basis. Many of the proposals embodied in the plan actually predate it, so that the NAP should be seen to some extent as incorporating aspects of existing policies. However it represents a new approach in some respects and there are key changes in emphasis which distinguish it from the OECD *Jobs Strategy*. In accordance with guidelines laid down by the EU, the plan, while emphasising youth employment, specifies numerical targets for an increase in employment up to 2002 and for a decline in the unemployment rate, and lays particular emphasis on equal opportunities. New EU guidelines are now being introduced to broaden the NAP to deal with the problem which most affects Austria, namely unemployment among older workers and the need to raise the employment rate in this group of the labour force.

Wage and work time flexibility have improved, and should remain on the agenda

Over the past year there has been further progress in a number of labour-market areas, while in some (*e.g.* university reform) progress has been slow and in others (such as competition policy) the need for policy initiatives has become more apparent and more pressing. As noted in the previous *Survey*, wage and work time flexibility have improved, partly as a result of the new labour time law, which has allowed the social partners to establish new patterns of work, and partly as a response to competitive pressures. Part-time work has increased rapidly, drawing women in particular into the labour force. However, the potential demand for opening clauses would seem to be wider than their use. Legal limits on working time in some occupations remain restrictive. Early retirement in one form or another remains important, thereby reducing the incentive for the needs of older workers to be taken into account in wage negotiations. More importantly, however, recent developments in the labour market have not been accepted fully by all, and there have been frequent demands to, *inter alia*, reduce the work week, lower overtime limits by legislation and give priority to federal wage agreements over regional and local ones. Although the NAP lends support to the need for modernising work organisation and for reforming employment contracts, exact measures will have to be worked out for achieving this. Reducing non-wage labour costs has been assigned the highest priority, but as noted, the scope for doing so by shifting the tax base to other factors is very limited.

The government should be responsible for creating the framework conditions for employment growth

Active labour market programmes have not been an important feature of policy but the NAP places great emphasis on them, in addition to plans to promote – and possibly subsidise – employment in the health sector and in social services. Experience in other countries suggests that the programmes will have to be very carefully chosen, focusing on promoting greater adaptability among the unemployed, so as not to crowd out private sector activity. Employment creation in the health and social sectors would have to be compatible with the need to improve efficiency in these sectors and to secure long-term financing. An increased reliance on active labour market measures in combination with numerical targets for employment creation should not be seen as implying that the government holds direct primary responsibility for labour market outcomes. Rather it should be responsible for creating the framework conditions and incentive signals under which the social partners work. This could be emphasised to a greater extent in the plan.

Austria has been successful in skill development, but modernisation has been required

The promotion of skills has been an important aspect of the Austrian success story and youth unemployment rates are comparatively low. However, the system of apprenticeships and full-time post-secondary training is under pressure from changing technology and market structure. The recent modernisation of the curricula for apprentices has been well received and could be continued at a more rapid pace. The new polytechnic institutions are also proving successful and the range of studies offered by them should be increased. Pressure is now on the government to stimulate the short-run demand for apprentices and special programmes have been set up for those who are most difficult to place, giving them the possibility to acquire qualifications at a more gradual pace than normal. Although the system is carefully targeted, monitoring will be required to ensure that the programme does not crowd-out other individuals from apprenticeships.

The innovation system requires improvement

Deficiencies in the innovation system have been apparent for quite some time. In response, the government has launched a "technology offensive" designed to address the problem with new programmes (*e.g.* to establish competence centres) and to raise the level of R&D spending. The programmes are now in place, and additional funding has been secured, although the envisaged organisational restructuring has been held back by institutional and political disputes. The innovation system clearly requires improvements. In a small open economy with significant foreign investment the object of government activity in this sphere should be to improve the adoption of new technologies by enhancing the absorptional capacity of enterprises and stimulating their capability to innovate, as well as to raise the ratio of R&D to GDP. To this end, the creation of an entrepreneurial climate where high-technology inputs are more fully disseminated and exploited is of great importance. In this respect, the university system appears to be a weak link in the innovation system, being characterised by low productivity and a lack of integration with the business sector. Further reforms to both the university budget system and the rules for academic promotion appear necessary in order to change incentive structures to encourage closer connection with the enterprise economy. This should involve both greater commercialisation of research and more active entrepreneurial behaviour on the part of graduates. Ongoing reform measures in the area need to be accelerated.

Product market opening should be completed and competition law enforcement improved

The promotion of product-market competition (*i.e.* maintaining open and contestable markets) is a key element of the *Jobs Strategy* and in this area some priorities are apparent. The recent political agreement on tightening the competition law should be seen as only the first step towards establishing an independent competition authority with powers to initiate actions. Recent cases of concentration or competitive abuse in Austria concerning retailing and the building industries indicate the limits of the consensual model in promoting competition when it is faced with conflicts of interest. This reform should be a priority. Also, despite recent reforms, the trades law (*Gewerbeordnung*) still maintains barriers to entry in a number of occupations and businesses (*e.g.* large surface retailing). In liberalising the law, attention should also be given to defining part-occupations (*Teilgewerbe*) and to increasing competition in the liberal professions. Other barriers are less formal: goods and services produced by the public sector should, as far as possible, be opened up to alternative suppliers. With respect to the network industries, significant progress has been made in opening up telecommunications and electricity to competition. However, prices for interconnecting with established networks remain a contentious issue which needs to be settled by keeping entry barriers as low and as transparent as possible, rather than on the basis of covering the sunk costs of the previous monopolist. In the electricity sector, market access should be granted in a non-discriminatory way which will require that the legal preference for generators in the public interest (*e.g.* environmentally-friendly generators) should only be granted in exceptional cases. Ensuring that product markets are open and competitive is a key element in fostering an efficient entrepreneurial environment.

Entrepreneurship needs to be fostered through better framework conditions

Entrepreneurship is fundamental to the dynamism and adaptability of an economy and as such has been emphasised both by the OECD *Jobs Strategy* and the NAP. Yet the fact that the concept is difficult to define makes the formulation of policy all the more difficult. Taking all the various aspects of entrepreneurship into account, it does appear that there is indeed a problem in Austria; despite a noticeable increase in the 1990s, the rate of start-ups is still low by international standards, although survival rates are relatively high. And although some firms have been exploiting new market opportunities in Europe, the economy appears to lack a large enough group of rapidly-growing enterprises to underpin growth prospects in the longer term. The taxation system might be a barrier here, making the take-over or inheritance of existing firms difficult. Key areas in this respect also concern the regulatory environment, the slowness and complexity of which appears to be a barrier to business activity, and the bankruptcy law which probably unnecessarily discourages risk taking by delaying the re-entry into business life of genuine entrepreneurs. In both areas there is great scope for improvement. The government's proposal to establish a "one-stop-shop" for regulatory approvals is an important step towards the establishment of better framework conditions, and should be accompanied by a more generalised process of deregulation to be fully effective.

Financial support for entrepreneurs should not encourage rent-seeking activity

There is often a tendency for the policy debate to focus on a lack of finance. Since bank loans are the dominant financing instrument for enterprises, Austrian capital markets remain rather underdeveloped. But the stock exchange is evolving and venture capital is developing, in part due to government initiatives, as is a network of "business angels". A take-over code has been introduced recently which protects the interests of minority shareholders. However, it needs to be stressed that lack of projects has probably been the major constraining factor in the past rather than the lack of finance. Direct government support programmes are now widespread and many encourage increased equity participation at some point. In such programmes it is important that the entrepreneur continues to bear a major part of the risks and that the focus is not on too narrow a definition of entrepreneurship: they should not be restricted to start-ups and the self employed, or relate only to high technology. Such financial programmes should not encourage entrepreneurs into rent-seeking activity.

Summing up

Summing up, the recent macroeconomic performance of the Austrian economy has been impressive, based on relatively rapid growth, low inflation and rising employment. With world trade slowing, the peak of the present business cycle seems to have passed, but wages, prices and productivity are projected to continue to develop favourably – in great part due to the major changes in the structure and operation of the economy in recent years. With macroeconomic policy supportive, medium-term prospects are sound. Looking ahead, the country nevertheless faces key challenges. The advent of the euro and continuing moves towards integration in Europe have reduced macroeconomic discretion, but underscored the need for fiscal consolidation. This is required in order to enhance the scope for budgetary manoeuvre and to free the resources needed to exploit the potential of the private sector, on which the economy has to rely for its dynamism. Establishing the full framework conditions for entrepreneurship to flourish requires, in addition to an effective system of containing public expenditures within the limits of the resources available, a more business-friendly and competition-enhancing regulatory environment and university reform. Difficult challenges remain in finding a consensus on these issues. However, if agreement can be found for moving forward in these areas, there is little doubt that the longer-run economic performance of the Austrian economy should continue to be very favourable.

I. Slowing growth in a favourable macroeconomic policy environment

Overview

When the Austrian economy was last reviewed in February 1998, short-term prospects were rather favourable with business sentiment improving, exports accelerating and household demand showing signs of recovery. Growth for 1998 was projected to be around $2^3/_4$ per cent rising to a little under 3 per cent in 1999. In the event, GDP expanded by some $3^1/_4$ per cent in 1998 driven by stronger than expected domestic demand and buoyant exports. However, the pattern of development throughout the year indicates that the peak of the present cycle may have been passed. GDP expanded rapidly in the first half of the year, but the business climate and expectations of export activity became significantly less optimistic in the course of the second half – and in particular following the Russian crisis in August – and this is likely to weaken investment activity. Since employment and real household disposable incomes have continued to increase and consumer sentiment has improved, domestic demand is projected to hold up, limiting the deceleration of activity. Fundamentals such as productivity and competitiveness are projected to remain sound and, with European inflation projected to remain low, monetary conditions are assumed to remain supportive so that growth should pick up again in 2000. Substantial risks are, however, associated with the development of international financial markets and the evolution of world trade.

The peak of the growth cycle has passed

Growth in 1998 was led by exports and investment

GDP expanded by an unexpectedly rapid 3.3 per cent in 1998, significantly above its estimated long term potential rate of growth, as domestic demand recovered (Figure 1). Investment in machinery and equipment was particularly robust, while construction activity was underpinned by strong demand

Figure 1. **Macroeconomic performance**[1]

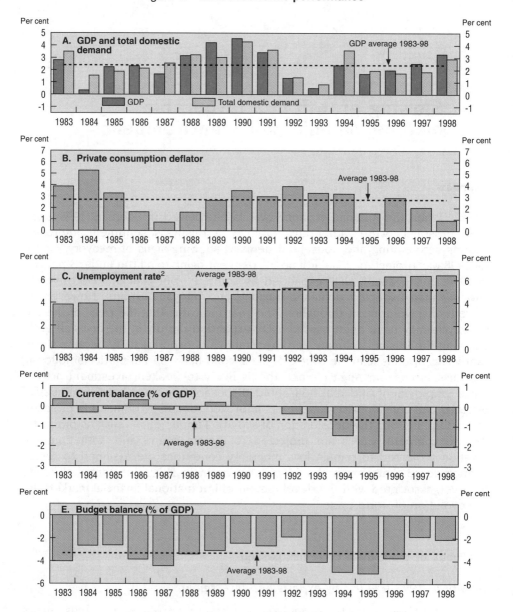

1.   1998 data are estimates.
2.   Registered unemployment as a per cent of total labour force, including self employment.
Source: OECD.

Table 1. **Demand and output**

Percentage change from previous year, constant 1983 prices

	1984-94 average	1995	1996	1997	1998[1]
Private consumption	2.2	2.9	2.0	0.7	1.8
Government consumption	1.6	–0.0	0.6	–3.9	1.5
Gross fixed investment	4.2	1.2	2.5	2.8	5.3
Construction	3.8	1.1	2.0	1.2	4.0
Machinery and equipment	4.9	1.3	3.1	4.9	7.0
Change in stocks[2]	0.0	0.0	–0.1	1.4	0.3
Total domestic demand	**2.6**	**1.9**	**1.7**	**1.8**	**2.9**
Exports of goods and services	5.0	6.5	6.9	10.1	7.5
of which: Goods	6.9	9.3	6.2	12.4	7.8
Imports of goods and services	5.5	7.0	6.3	8.7	6.8
of which: Goods	6.5	3.9	5.4	9.1	7.2
Foreign balance[2]	–0.2	–0.3	0.2	0.7	0.4
Gross domestic product	**2.4**	**1.7**	**2.0**	**2.5**	**3.3**
Memorandum items :					
GDP price deflator	3.1	2.3	1.7	1.6	1.2
Private consumption deflator	2.9	1.5	2.9	2.0	0.9
Unemployment rate					
Registered[3]	4.9	5.9	6.3	6.4	6.4
Eurostat	. .	3.9	4.3	4.4	4.4

1. Partly estimated.
2. Contribution to change in GDP (as a percentage of real GDP in the previous period).
3. As a percentage of the total labour force including self-employment.
Source: OECD.

for apartment renovation which was stimulated by the need to use tax free reserves by the end of 1998 (since extended to the end of 1999) in order to avoid taxation. Private and public consumption also recovered from the low rates of growth associated with fiscal consolidation in 1997 (Table 1).[1] Export growth was rapid but the net contribution to growth remained about the same as in 1997.

The terms of trade improved during 1998 and, with receipts from tourism rising, the current account deficit declined by some Sch 8 billion, falling from around 2.4 per cent of GDP to some 2 per cent (Table 2). Sharply lower prices of raw materials on world markets were also reflected in pressure on export prices for basic goods which are important for Austria. Overall, export prices remained constant in 1998, while import prices declined by around 1 per cent. These price developments were reflected in manufactured prices in the consumer price index, which remained stable while the rate of increase in food prices declined significantly (Figure 2). Broader forces have also been at work with service price inflation stabilising at 1 per cent although rents have increased at a faster pace. Overall, both the consumer price index and the deflator rose by a remarkably low 1 per cent, with the year-on-year rate during the year even more favourable.

Table 2. **Current account of the balance of payments**

Billion schillings

	1992	1993	1994	1995	1996	1997	1998
Goods and services	18.7	12.5	−6.2	−20.6	−28.9	−39.2	−17.3
Merchandise	−84.1	−75.3	−90.2	−67.0	−77.0	−52.0	−50.8
Exports	488.8	468.4	513.8	581.4	613.9	716.1	772.0
Imports	572.9	543.7	604.0	648.5	690.9	768.0	822.8
Services, net	102.8	87.8	84.0	46.5	48.2	12.7	33..5
of which: Travel	64.3	58.1	39.5	26.5	18.6	10.8	20.7
Exports	151.0	148.5	139.9	136.0	135.3	134.1	139.2
Imports	86.7	90.4	100.4	109.5	116.7	123.2	118.5
Investment income, net	−15.6	−12.4	−14.6	−16.2	−3.1	−1.4	−13.1
Transfers, net	−11.1	−11.7	−12.3	−17.3	−18.8	−20.7	−24.0
Official	−6.7	−7.8	−8.3	−14.3	−15.5	−18.8	−18.6
Private	−4.3	−3.9	−4.0	−3.0	−3.3	−1.9	−5.4
Current account	−8.0	−11.7	−33.1	−54.0	−50.8	−61.4	−54.5
Per cent of GDP	−0.4	−0.5	−1.5	−2.3	−2.1	−2.4	−2.1

Source: Austrian National Bank.

Private consumption has been supported by rising household incomes

Private consumption has been stimulated by rising household disposable income although, as in the past, faster income growth has been used to restore savings eroded during the period of consolidation and slow growth: the household savings ratio has risen.[2] In contrast to the business sector, consumer confidence remained favourable throughout 1998 and consumer expenditures remained robust entering 1999. Key to the revival of household income has been the steady growth of employment (Figure 3, panel A), together with effective wage increases of some 2 per cent, so that labour incomes rose by 3 per cent. At the same time, fiscal levies stabilised following the large increase in 1997, while lower inflation also served to raise real incomes.

Moderate wage increases, rising productivity and a shift in the composition of demand to more labour-intensive domestic components were factors behind the increase in employment, and the number of unfilled vacancies also rose (Figure 3, panel B). Employment growth has been particularly strong in services and in retailing and has mainly been in the form of part-time jobs. Around two-thirds of the increase of employment has been accounted for by women as many have re-entered the labour force. Institutional factors associated with changing entitlements to maternity leave have also contributed to the pick up in the female labour force participation. This trend has offset the inflows into early retirement which are still high, so that the number of registered

Figure 2.   **Consumer price inflation**
Percentage changes from year ago

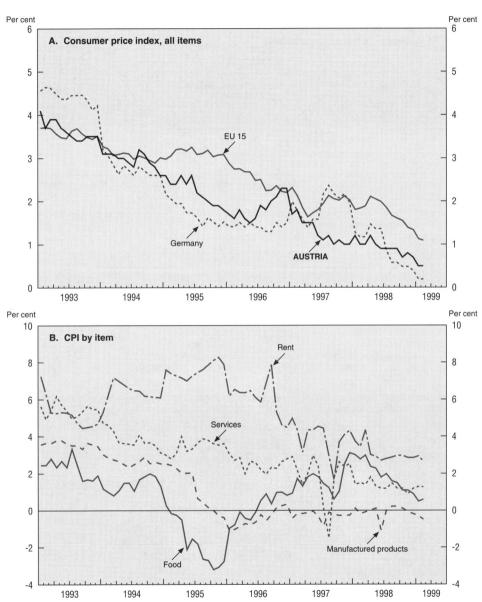

Source: Austrian Institute for Economic Research (WIFO); OECD, *Main Economic Indicators*.

Figure 3. **Employment, unemployment and the labour force**
Seasonally adjusted

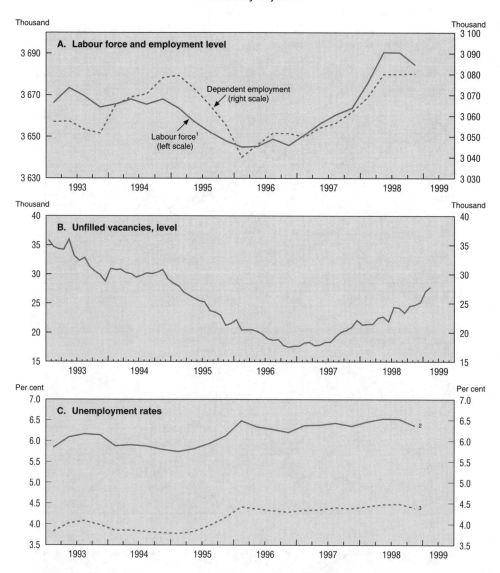

1. 1998 quarterly data for the labour force are based on an annual estimation of self employment data for 1998.
2. Registered unemployment as a per cent of total labour force, including self employment.
3. Labour force survey.
Source: WIFO; OECD, *Main Economic Indicators.*

unemployed actually rose by some five thousand and the unemployment rate remained broadly stable at 7.2 per cent of dependent employment or 4.4 per cent of the labour force on the basis of the standardised definition (Figure 3, panel C).

Growth slowed in the second half as business sentiment has deteriorated

Activity slowed markedly in the second half of 1998 having expanded rapidly in the first half: in the first and second quarters of 1998, GDP is estimated to have grown by over 4 per cent (year-on-year) but in the second half growth slowed to 2½ per cent.[3] Growth was driven by surging exports and by strong investment activity in the first half. With import growth temporarily lagging and the tourism balance improving, real net exports contributed significantly to the growth of output and the current account improved. However, reflecting slowing world trade, export growth decelerated markedly in the second half and this was reflected in slower growth rates in manufacturing: whereas exports grew at double digit rates in the first half, in the third quarter nominal exports were only up 7 per cent on a year earlier while manufacturing growth subsided from 9½ per cent (nominal) in the first quarter to 5 per cent in July and August (year-on-year). Private consumption appears to have remained buoyant up until the end of the year although employment (seasonally-adjusted) levelled off from May onwards. Investment in machinery and equipment also remained strong and apartment renovation flourished, although new apartment and housing construction have fallen significantly since the summer.

The business climate weakened throughout 1998, especially in the last quarter, to levels last seen at the start of 1995, although some stabilisation became discernable in early 1999. Production and capacity utilisation indicators followed suit (Figure 4). At the same time, there appears to have been an increase in stocks of finished goods, which often indicates pressure to reduce production in the future. The deterioration in the business climate has mirrored the steady deceleration in incoming foreign manufacturing orders following the deceleration of world trade in the wake of the Asian crisis. The Russian crisis in August 1998 acted as an additional factor in depressing the environment even though Russia is not a particularly important trading partner: Russia's share of Austrian exports was 1½ per cent and those to Asia including Japan 6¼ per cent in 1997.

Monetary conditions and forces acting on the economy

Competitiveness remains sound with wage and price developments favourable

A strengthening of the schilling *vis-à-vis* the US dollar in the second half of 1998, together with the currency depreciations in Asia and other emerging

Figure 4. **The climate in the business sector**

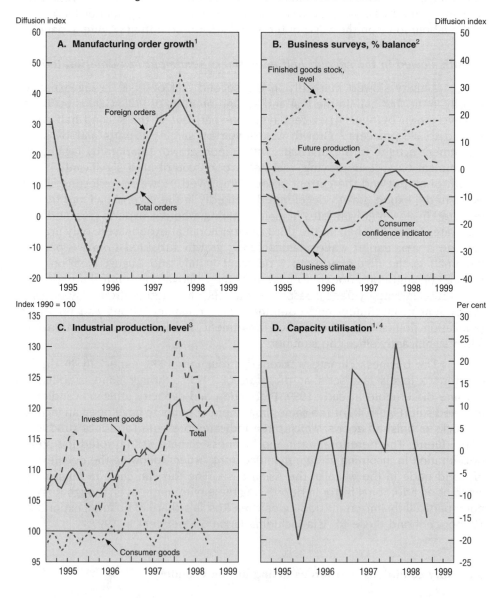

1. Balance of positive – negative replies.
2. Seasonally adjusted. Balance of positive – negative replies.
3. 3-month moving average.
4. *Industrievereinigung.*
Source: WIFO; OECD, *Main Economic Indicators.*

markets, meant that the nominal effective exchange rate appreciated to some extent in 1998, although it remains at virtually the same level as in 1995. For the economy as a whole, unit labour costs were broadly stable as productivity growth was matched by wage increases, while in manufacturing, which is subject to more intense international pressure, unit labour costs have continued to decline (Table 3). Measured in terms of relative unit labour costs in manufacturing, the real exchange rate has thus declined significantly over the last three years (Figure 5). The autumn wage round has by and large set a pattern for moderate increases in 1999 and the public sector has settled for 2½ per cent. The agreement in the metal industry for increases of some 3½ per cent was high in view of the expected slowing of industrial activity,[4] but other sectors have settled for increases more in the range of 2¾ per cent. From the cost side there do not appear to be any prospective pressures either on inflation which, as noted above, has fallen to a level close to price level stability, or on international competitiveness.

Monetary conditions are favourable for growth

Monetary policy during the transition to the euro

Overall, monetary conditions have generally been favourable for growth during the past year and, in view of low inflation and falling interest rates, the stance of European monetary policy seems set to remain expansionary until well into 2000.[5] During 1998 interest rates were influenced by two sets of factors: the need to ensure a smooth run up to the introduction of the euro and the turmoil on financial markets, which has led to a marked flight to quality, particularly since the crisis in Russia. The credibility of Austrian monetary policy in particular, and of arrangements for the introduction of the euro in general, have been demonstrated by the fact that no pressures on the exchange rate emerged over the period, while the long term interest rate declined in line with the German 10-year rate. As a result, real long term interest rates (however measured) are now at their lowest levels since the 1970s. Although the yield curve has also flattened, this probably cannot be taken as signalling restrictive conditions: it has been caused by falling long rates rather than rising short rates. Credit by the banking sector to domestic non-banks including the public sector expanded by only 3½ per cent in 1998. But lending to domestic households and firms is still buoyant (growing by some 6 per cent) and there are no signs of credit restrictions on the part of banks. Despite the large direct exposure of the banking system to Russia and to other emerging markets – as in other countries, the indirect exposure is not known with any precision – bank capital remains adequate to support continued lending activity.

Throughout 1998, monetary policy was guided by the need to ensure a smooth transition to the euro. As in Germany, policy-controlled interest rates in

Table 3. **Wages and prices**

Annual growth, per cent

	1984-94	1995	1996	1997	1998[1]
Productivity per employee, total economy	1.7	2.1	2.7	2.3	2.6
Compensation per employee, total economy	4.7	3.6	2.0	0.9	2.4
Unit labour costs, total economy	3.3	1.8	-0.7	-1.3	-0.2
Compensation per employee, business sector	5.0	3.5	2.0	3.0	2.3
Unit labour costs, business sector	2.9	1.0	-1.0	1.5	-0.5
Wages in industry,[2] hourly rates	5.1	3.7	3.3	2.4	n.a.
Unit labour costs, manufacturing	0.3	-1.1	-1.0	-5.2	-3.5
GDP deflator	3.1	2.3	1.7	1.6	1.2
Private consumption deflator	2.9	1.5	2.9	2.0	0.9

1. 1998 partly estimated.
2. Industry, including construction and electricity.
Source: OECD; WIFO.

Figure 5. **Indicators of competitiveness**

Index 1991 = 100

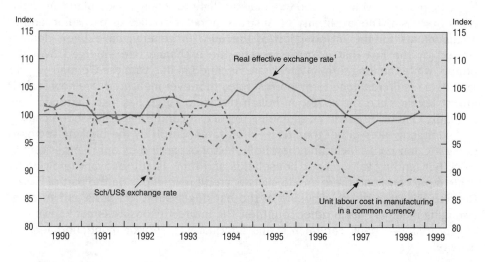

1. Deflated by the CPI.
Source: OECD, *Main Economic Indicators*; OECD.

Austria remained low and unchanged until December. On 3 December the central banks participating in EMU, in a co-ordinated action and in agreement with the ECB, lowered their key policy rates to 3 per cent.[6] The central banks made it clear that this level should be the entry rate for the euro and it was seen to be consistent with both monetary stability and an appropriate response to the conjunctural risks arising from the turmoil on world financial markets. In line with this decision, the National Bank (OeNB) reduced the rate for the two-week volume tender by 20 basis points. This was 10 basis points less than the reduction of the repurchasing rate by the Deutsche Bundesbank, reflecting the fact that the Austrian rate had been lower since August 1997.[7] In a complementary move one week later, the OeNB reduced the *Gomex*-rate for short-term open market operations by 20 basis points.

Money market rates tended to remain stable throughout 1998, fluctuating within a relatively narrow band. Convergence of short-term rates in the prospective euro area accelerated in the second half, driven by the scheduled conversion of national currencies to the euro and supported by policy rate cuts in countries with initially higher levels. By November 1998, convergence of short term rates in the prospective euro area was largely completed at the lower end of the interest rate spectrum which included Austria. During this process the differential between Austrian and German 3-month rates, which had moved in tandem since mid-1997, narrowed further to less than 10 basis points (Figure 6, panels B and C).

Following a nine month period of consistently falling bond yields in 1997 (Figure 6, panel A), capital market rates continued their downward trend in 1998; indeed, by December 1998 the spread between 3-month rates and those for 10-year government bonds, which had been 100 basis points in January, had disappeared. Yields declined throughout the year apart from a temporary recovery in April and May. The decline was particularly pronounced for long-term bonds with 10-year bond yields falling by 1.3 percentage points between December 1997 and December 1998 to 3.6 per cent, the lowest level for ten years. A major factor behind these movements, which were in line with those in Germany, was the general "flight to quality" in the wake of turbulence in Asia and elsewhere: capital inflows were strong (Table 4). Other factors also seem likely to have contributed to the rise in bond prices. With expectations about the introduction and membership of the euro becoming firmer, domestic inflation virtually coming to a halt and import prices declining, inflation expectations were probably being revised downwards.

Policy implementation under the euro

On 1 January 1999 the conversion rate of the schilling into the euro was set at Sch 13.7603 per euro and the responsibility for setting monetary policy shifted to the European Central Bank (ECB). As a member of the European

Figure 6. **Interest rate developments**

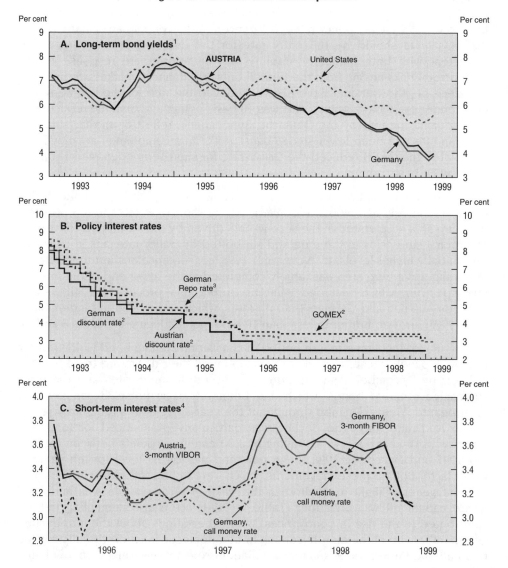

1. Austria: 10-year benchmark bond; Germany: yields on listed federal securities with residual maturities of 9 to 10 years; United States: US Government bonds (composite over 10 years).
2. Ended in December 1998.
3. From January 1999 EURO Repo rate.
4. From January 1999 VIBOR and FIBOR have been replaced by EURIBOR; call money rates have been replaced by EONIA.
Source: Oesterreichische Nationalbank; Deutsche Bundesbank; OECD, *Main Economic Indicators.*

Table 4. **Capital account of the balance of payments**

Billion schillings

	1992	1993	1994	1995	1996	1997	1998
Current balance	−8.0	−11.7	−33.1	−54.0	−50.8	−61.4	−54.5
Balance of capital transfers and financial transactions	−2.6	15.1	35.8	58.9	44.7	55.2	53.1
of which:							
Balance of financial transactions	−2.1	20.3	36.8	59.5	43.8	54.9	55.1
Direct investment	−2.9	−0.6	9.7	7.8	26.4	5.3	35.9
Austrian abroad	18.7	13.8	14.4	11.4	20.5	23.8	37.3
Foreign in Austria	15.7	13.2	24.0	19.2	46.9	29.1	73.2
Portfolio investment in shares and investment certificates	−0.1	6.6	4.1	5.7	18.2	2.4	−60.8
Austrian abroad	1.8	7.3	11.0	6.8	10.0	32.4	72.2
Foreign in Austria	1.7	13.8	15.0	12.5	28.2	34.8	11.4
Portfolio investment in fixed-interest securities	70.5	63.8	−6.9	88.4	−44.9	11.5	111.9
Foreign securities	27.9	14.9	41.5	23.0	75.8	91.1	80.2
Domestic securities	98.4	78.7	34.6	111.4	30.9	102.6	192.1
Other financial transactions	−41.8	−22.9	40.6	−28.6	55.3	−0.3	8.2
Claims on foreigners	80.3	59.1	31.8	102.0	−9.0	63.3	22.1
Claims on domestic residents	38.5	36.2	72.4	73.4	46.4	63.1	30.4
Changes in official reserves	−27.8	−26.5	−10.6	−13.8	−11.1	35.9	−40.1
Errors and omissions	10.6	−3.4	−2.7	−4.9	6.1	6.2	1.3

Source: Austrian National Bank.

System of Central Banks, the OeNB will participate in the formulation of monetary policy for the euro zone, whereas under the "hard-currency" link to the Deutsche-mark the OeNB was constrained to follow Bundesbank policy moves. The OeNB also assumes the task of implementing policy in Austria.[8] Both the Oester-reichische Nationalbank and the financial sector had already adapted their operations to the monetary policy framework adopted by the European System of Central Banks (ESCB) (see *Economic Survey*, 1998). This contributed to a smooth transition to the euro. Repurchase tenders with a two week maturity, which now constitute the most important refinancing instrument of the ESCB, have been the most important OeNB instrument for managing the liquidity of the banking sector and for signalling the stance of monetary policy since the end of 1995. The OeNB has also utilised standing facilities to provide overnight liquidity, a policy instrument which is applied by the ESCB as well ("marginal lending facility"). There is also an additional deposit facility which was not available in the previous system.[9] The conditions for minimum reserves were streamlined during the last few years to better conform with the practices within the EU. These reserves will now be remunerated to avoid market distortions.[10]

Short-term prospects and risks

While activity has slowed going into 1999, the economy remains fundamentally sound, with wage, price and productivity developments favourable to continued moderate growth. With both real interest rates and actual and expected inflation low, monetary conditions in the euro area are expected to remain supportive of growth through 1999 and 2000. Fiscal policy has become more neutral since the squeeze of 1996-97 and this stance is expected to continue in 1999.

The growth deceleration should be limited

Against this policy background, GDP growth is projected to slow in 1999 to around 2¼ per cent as exports remain weak and investment adjusts to lower world demand but, given the favourable fundamentals outlined above, domestic demand should limit the extent of the slow down (Table 5). Reflecting the

Table 5. **Economic projections to 2000**

Percentage change from previous year, constant 1983 prices

	1998	1999	2000
Private consumption	1.8	2.0	2.1
Government consumption	1.5	1.5	1.5
Gross fixed investment	5.3	3.6	4.3
Construction	4.0	2.5	2.8
Machinery and equipment	7.0	5.0	6.0
Change in stocks[1]	0.3	0.0	0.0
Total domestic demand	2.9	2.3	2.5
Exports of goods and services	7.5	4.0	5.6
Imports of goods and services	6.8	4.2	5.5
Foreign balance[1]	0.4	−0.1	0.1
Gross domestic product	3.3	2.2	2.6
Memorandum items:			
Private consumption deflator	0.9	0.7	1.2
GDP price deflator	1.2	1.0	1.4
Total employment[2]	0.7	0.3	0.3
Unemployment rate (registered)	6.4	6.3	6.1
Household saving ratio, level	8.6	9.1	9.7
Export market growth[3]	8.3	3.4	5.9
Short-term interest rate	3.6	2.7	2.6
Long-term interest rate	4.7	4.1	4.2
General government budget balance, per cent of GDP	−2.1	−2.2	−2.1
Current balance, per cent of GDP	−2.0	−2.1	−2.1

1.   Contributions to changes in GDP (as a percentage of real GDP in the previous period).
2.   Including self employment.
3.   Manufactured goods.
Source: OECD, April 1999.

deterioration in the business climate and in exports, growth could be particularly slow in the first half, but should recover in the course of the year. With respect to domestic demand, investment is projected to soften somewhat, but to remain significantly underpinned by expenditure on machinery and equipment. The housing sector is already showing signs of weakness and construction could weaken further as renovation expenditures start to decline. The requirement to use certain financial reserves for renovation or to pay taxes, which was originally to expire at the end of 1998, has been extended through 1999, but it is likely that the bulk of the reserves have already been used. Despite slowing employment growth, consumer demand is projected to grow moderately by some 2 per cent, supported by rising real household disposable incomes. In line with past patterns, the household savings ratio is also projected to rise somewhat.

Growth is projected to recover in 2000 to around $2\frac{1}{2}$ per cent, close to long-run potential, on the basis of a pick-up in world export markets. The recovery should be underpinned by strong macroeconomic fundamentals: wages, prices, productivity and the macro policy environment are all projected to remain favourable to continued growth. Although the output gap is projected to decline over the projection period, it will not be sufficient to lead to a significant pick-up in inflation. At the same time, world raw material prices are assumed to remain depressed since global activity is only projected to recover gradually.

... but there are significant downside risks

The projections assume that turbulence in world financial markets will not adversely affect consumer sentiment or significantly lower planned corporate investment. There is, however, considerable uncertainty about how instability in the international environment might be transmitted to the domestic economy, and more negative outcomes via depressed business sentiment cannot be excluded. Downside risks to the projection would arise if activity in surrounding countries, including Germany where the business climate has deteriorated markedly, were to be weaker than projected as a result of the instability.[11] From a domestic perspective, some uncertainty for the projection arises from the steady build up in inventories which could lead to a sharper than projected slowdown in early 1999. The downside risks, however, should be kept in perspective. In the event of major risks developing which would affect Europe as a whole, monetary policy in the euro area would probably adjust, while fiscal policy would allow automatic stabilisers to work, at least in the short run. However, fiscal policy would not seem to have a great deal of room for manœuvre in the case of a more protracted slowdown and these issues are discussed in the following chapter.

II. Fiscal policy: consolidation and reform

Bringing the budget deficit down to a level consistent with the Maastricht Treaty has been a major accomplishment for Austria's budgetary strategy, which has now turned to ensuring that the deficit will remain below the 3 per cent limit under "normal" business cycle conditions. The pressure to meet the conditions for EMU entry has brought significant structural reforms to the budget process, which in the short run should ensure sufficient institutional control over public spending for this objective to be realised. However, the pace of consolidation has slowed since 1997, and the projected decline of the general government deficit over the next three years is quite modest. This would still seem to leave the budget balance vulnerable to the dangers that social spending pressures and/or any sustained conjunctural weakness could cause an overshooting, demanding a higher level of fiscal ambition.

Completing the fiscal consolidation process

The 1997 budget: a successful outturn

To ensure that Austria would meet the Maastricht deficit criterion for participation in European Economic and Monetary Union (EMU), the fiscal consolidation packages enacted in 1996 and 1997 needed to bring the general government budget deficit down below 3 per cent of GDP from the excessive level of 5 per cent reached in 1995. The actual outturn was 1.9 per cent of GDP (Table 6), the bulk of the consolidation emanating from a swing from primary deficit to surplus. In addition, debt sales, privatisation and the removal of quasi-commercial government entities (i.e. those with at least 50 per cent of income derived from market activities) from the federal budget were significant in reducing the gross debt/GDP ratio from around 70 to 64½ per cent of GDP.

Consolidation was achieved against the background of weakening economic activity and shortfalls in revenues and contributions, which were counteracted by curbs on public spending. At the federal level a Sch 5 billion shortfall in revenues (prior to tax sharing) coincided with a Sch 10½ billion overrun in

Table 6. **Net lending of the general government**[1]

National accounts basis, billions of schillings

	1995	1996	1997	1998	1999	2000
Current receipts	1 106.6	1 159.9	1 206.0	1 243.0	1 278.8	1 325.0
Total direct taxes	327.7	363.8	386.4	407.7	416.8	428.2
Households	286.5	306.1	331.2	344.6	357.3	367.3
Business	41.2	57.7	55.3	63.1	59.5	60.8
Total indirect taxes	341.0	358.6	380.3	395.6	410.6	427.9
Social security and other current transfers received	387.1	394.9	403.7	411.5	425.3	442.1
Property and entrepreneurial income	50.9	42.6	35.5	28.2	26.0	26.9
Current disbursements	1 130.0	1 155.2	1 178.6	1 217.3	1 255.6	1 297.9
Government consumption	469.4	480.3	478.2	494.6	512.0	530.6
of which: Wages and salaries	298.4	301.7	262.6	269.2	277.3	285.6
Interest on public debt	102.4	105.9	100.8	105.5	105.7	107.3
Subsidies	60.6	56.2	62.4	61.5	63.0	63.6
Social security and other current transfers paid	526.6	544.4	549.4	570.2	591.9	617.2
Net capital outlays	95.2	95.0	74.7	81.1	83.1	85.0
Gross investment	66.1	68.3	49.3	53.8	56.0	58.2
Net capital transfers paid and other capital transactions	−44.8	−43.0	−42.0	−44.5	−44.8	−45.0
Less: Consumption of fixed capital	15.7	16.2	16.7	17.2	17.7	18.2
Net lending	−118.6	−90.4	−47.2	−55.5	−59.9	−57.9
(As a percentage of GDP)	−5.1	−3.7	−1.9	−2.1	−2.2	−2.0
Gross debt (Maastricht basis)						
(As a percentage of GDP)	69.4	69.8	64.4	63.1	63.1	62.7
Structural budget balance						
(As a percentage of potential GDP)	−4.4	−3.1	−1.3	−2.0	−2.1	−2.0

1.   From 1998 onwards, OECD projections.
Source: OECD, April 1999.

transfers to the social security system, consisting mainly of federal contributions to the public pension scheme. This was more than compensated by a larger-than-budgeted decline in interest payments, related to lower interest rates, and in current and capital spending on goods. The marked drop in investment outlays, which were cut in half in comparison to the 1996 outcome, is mainly attributable to the Post Office being moved off-budget (Table 7).

Overall, the government spending/GDP ratio was reduced by 1¾ per cent of GDP in 1997 and by a cumulative 2¾ per cent from 1995 to 1997. Community budgets were helped by spinning-off units with commercial activities into the public enterprise sector, which contributed to the cut in communal investment

Table 7. **The Federal budget**

Cash basis, adjusted; billions of schillings

	1995 Outturn	1996 Outturn	1997 Budget	1997 Outturn	1998 Budget	1998 Expected outturn	1999 Budget
Revenue [1]	584.3	604.7	635.7	630.6	640.6	655.9	652.2
(Percentage change) [2]	(+0.7)	(+3.5)	(+5.2)	(+4.3)	(+0.1)	(+4.0)	(+1.8)
Taxes before revenue sharing	521.2	585.7	631.6	623.9	667.7	670.2	681.1
Wage tax	150.2	160.5	183.3	183.6	188.0	193.7	198.0
Taxes on other income and profits	61.0	80.7	89.0	86.5	88.2	94.3	90.0
Value-added tax	179.9	204.1	213.0	207.2	223.0	216.3	233.0
Major excise taxes [3]	43.7	48.5	47.2	47.9	50.0	50.7	50.5
Other taxes	86.4	91.9	99.1	98.8	118.5	115.2	109.6
Minus tax-sharing transfers	156.6	175.3	178.4	179.2	184.9	183.8	192.7
Minus transfers to EU budget	18.8	26.9	30.1	31.6	30.2	26.2	31.5
Taxes after revenue sharing	345.8	383.5	423.2	413.2	452.6	460.2	456.9
Tax transfers to federal funds [4]	19.7	19.5	19.8	19.6	20.0	19.6	20.5
Tax-like revenue	82.6	84.1	87.8	85.7	87.0	89.1	90.5
Federal enterprises	65.1	25.7	0.7	0.7	0.7	0.8	0.4
Other revenue	71.1	91.9	104.2	111.3	80.4	86.2	83.9
Expenditure	710.2	696.9	704.4	695.3	709.1	711.1	726.9
(Percentage change) [2]	(+4.5)	(-1.9)	(+1.1)	(-0.2)	(+0.2)	(+2.3)	(+2.5)
Wages and salaries [5]	140.3	137.7	134.3	137.0	138.8	140.7	142.0
Pensions [6]	48.8	42.7	39.8	39.1	40.1	39.6	43.1
Current expenditure on goods [7]	66.5	64.5	65.6	62.2	67.1	65.2	65.7
Gross investment	25.5	20.8	12.5	10.3	11.3	10.6	10.9
Transfer payments	320.7	322.4	335.0	336.3	346.5	348.0	354.3
Family allowances	57.5	56.5	53.8	54.3	51.5	51.0	54.0
Unemployment benefits	32.8	34.6	35.6	32.9	32.9	33.8	32.8
Transfers to the social security system [8]	86.9	92.4	86.7	97.3	102.2	103.7	103.6
Transfers to enterprises [9]	45.3	52.7	59.9	55.4	57.7	56.6	60.0
Other transfers [10]	98.2	86.2	99.0	96.3	102.2	102.9	103.8
Interest [11]	84.1	88.5	94.8	88.7	92.5	91.3	98.6
Other expenditure	24.4	20.3	22.4	21.7	12.7	15.7	12.3
Net balance	-125.9	-92.2	-68.7	-64.7	-68.5	-55.2	-74.7
(in per cent of GDP)	(5.4)	(3.8)	(2.8)	(2.6)	(2.6)	(2.1)	(2.7)
Memorandum item:							
Net balance, administrative basis	-117.9	-89.4	-68.0	-67.2	-67.3	-66.0	-70.1
(in per cent of GDP)	(5.0)	(3.7)	(2.7)	(2.7)	(2.6)	(2.5)	(2.6)

1. Adjusted for double counting.
2. For outturn: over last year's outturn; for budget: over last year's budget.
3. Mineral oil and tobacco taxes.
4. Mainly contributions to unemployment insurance and to the fund for family allowances.
5. Including contributions to salaries of teachers employed by the states.
6. Pensions of federal civil servants and contribution to pensions of teachers employed by the states.
7. Including investment expenditure on defence.
8. Mainly the general pension system (ASVG; Sch 68.7 billion in the 1997 expected outturn).
9. Including agriculture.
10. Including transfers to other levels of government; as of 1995, also including operations related to EU accession.
11. Including commissions and management fees and provision for interest on zero-bonds; excluding interest on swap transactions.

Source: Ministry of Finance.

Table 8. **Budget deficit by government level**

National accounts basis, billions of schillings

	1993	1994	1995	1996	1997	1998
Federal government	−101.4	−109.0	−112.7	−100.4	−64.5	−67.0
States (excluding Vienna)	15.6	6.3	3.8	10.1	11.2	9.4
Communities (including Vienna)	−3.7	−9.5	−8.7	−2.3	2.3	0.4
Social security funds	0.2	1.3	−0.9	2.3	3.7	1.7
General government	−89.4	−110.9	−118.6	−90.4	−47.2	−55.4
(As a percentage of GDP)	−4.2	−5.0	−5.1	−3.7	−1.9	−2.1

Note: − = deficit
Source: Ministry of Finance.

and reduced the general government deficit by some Sch 4.5 billion overall. The social security system also produced a surplus of 0.1 per cent of GDP and was mainly attributable to health care reforms enacted in 1997 which led to savings in the hospital and ambulatory sectors as well as to lower outlays for sick leave (Table 8).

1998: a budgetary pause

Following the rapid consolidation of 1997, the 1998 budget targeted a further small reduction in the general government deficit to 2.2 per cent of GDP (from a 1997 figure initially put at 2.5 per cent). The actual deficit came in at 2.1 per cent of GDP, with the federal government incurring a deficit of 2.5 per cent (Tables 6 and 8). While the outcome may have been as expected, the deficit actually rose in comparison to the 1997 outturn, despite the fact that the growth of nominal GDP and employment exceeded the 1998 budget projections. This lends support to estimates by the OECD of a structural budget deficit around 2 per cent of GDP. Wage tax receipts and social security contributions benefited from improved growth while profit taxes also turned out to be greater than expected, reflecting the lagged effects of both higher profits in past years and tax measures contained in the 1996 tax reform package (abolition of preferential tax treatments, increase in tax pre-payments). General government expenditures, on the other hand, increased by 3½ per cent, after a growth of 0.2 per cent in 1997. Both the Länder and community spending picked up, public consumption rising by more than 5 per cent, although the wage bill developed moderately. Public investment also recovered.

Regarding the federal budget outcome, the deficit was about Sch 1 billion lower than planned. But the improvement was entirely due to unexpectedly stronger revenues, which, on an administrative basis, exceeded the budget projections by about Sch 25 billion (Table 7). On the spending side, unemployment related outlays were higher than budgeted. This was mainly attributable to the expansion in active labour market measures introduced in spring 1998 in accordance with the National Action Plan for Employment (NAP) (see Chapter III below). In addition, transfers to the Labour Office (*Arbeitsmarktservice*) increased due to higher-than-expected unemployment (registered unemployment totalled 7.2 per cent – national definition – rather than 6.9 per cent projected for the budget). Important overruns also occurred with respect to other social transfers and outlays for personnel.

The 1999 budget: no further improvement

As was the case for 1996-97, the federal budgets for 1998 and 1999 were formulated on a biennial basis, although that for 1999 was legislated only in 1998. The original fiscal policy objective was to reduce the general government deficit/GDP ratio by a quarter of a point of GDP each year. The programme was based on projected overall savings of some Sch 27 billion against the 1997 baseline. About two-thirds of the savings are allocated on the spending side in terms of lower outlays for personnel and reductions in social transfers, the remainder stems from revenue-raising measures. While the savings programme is still valid, and was restated in the Stability Programme submitted by the government in November 1998 to the EU Commission,[12] the overall spending profile has been overridden to some extent in favour of higher outlays due to new demands.

A revision of the family benefit system became necessary due to a ruling of the Constitutional Court in October 1997, which found the existing system of family taxation unconstitutional in that it did not sufficiently differentiate between families with and without children. The Court argued that at least half the subsistence expenses for children should be tax free. After consultations with the social partners and between the coalition parties, the government responded by a general increase in per-child benefits, phased in two steps over 1999 and 2000. For 1999 this implies an additional budgetary burden of Sch 6 billion in terms of both extended tax credits and cash benefits paid from the Family Equalisation Fund (*Familienlastenausgleichsfonds*). By 2000 the full-year cost will be Sch 12 billion. Also, the National Action Plan for Employment requires additional budgetary resources of Sch 4.4 billion in 1999, of which Sch 1.5 billion consists of an additional transfer to the Labour Office for the purpose of strengthening active labour market policies. The government plans to finance the largest part of NAP induced spending *via* budget shifts from other programmes.

Incorporating these initiatives, overall federal expenditures are budgeted to increase by 2.5 per cent in relation to the 1998 budget. Although federal personnel (*Planstellen*) are scheduled to be cut by 1 per cent, wages and salaries are budgeted to increase by 2½ per cent. Central government current expenditure

Figure 7. **General government budget balances**[1]
Per cent of GDP

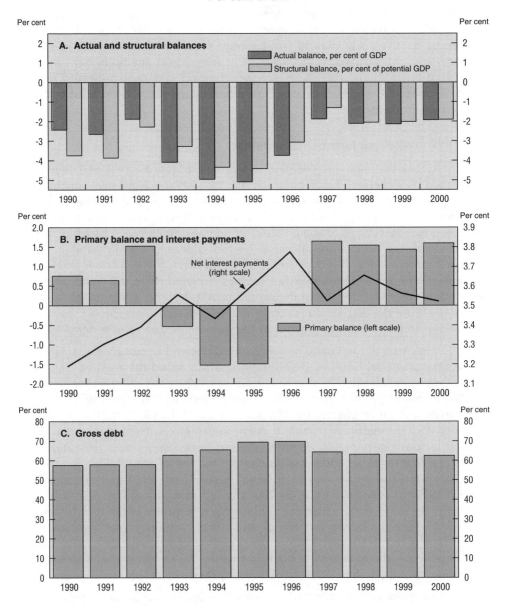

on goods is set to decline in nominal terms. But transfer payments are budgeted to increase due to the increase in family allowances (4.9 per cent) and higher subsidies to enterprises. There are no new policy changes on the revenue side (apart from extended tax credits for families). In national accounts terms the central government deficit is officially projected to amount to 2.5 per cent of GDP in 1999.

At the general government level, the deficit-to-GDP ratio is projected by the government to fall to 2 per cent, based on real GDP growth of 2.8 per cent[13] and a decline of the unemployment rate to 7.0 per cent (national definition). Based on a slower growth outlook (growth of 2¼ per cent), the OECD projects an unchanged deficit of 2.1 per cent of GDP (Table 6) and no change in the cyclically-adjusted deficit which remains at around 2 per cent. The primary surplus suffices to stabilise government gross debt in terms of GDP (Figure 7).

On current policies the government projects a further small decline in the general government deficit to 1.7 per cent of GDP in 2000. Implementation of the second adjustment of the family support scheme implies a further budgetary burden of Sch 6 billion. According to the OECD assessment, which for 2000 projects a similar GDP growth rate as the government, the deficit is projected to amount to 2 per cent of GDP, with the structural balance also projected to remain at around 2 per cent.[14] The debt-to-GDP ratio is projected to fall by ½ percentage point (assuming that there are no further debt adjustments due to asset sales or revaluations).

The medium-term fiscal stabilisation plan

According to the 1998 Stability Programme, Austria aims at reducing the general government deficit up to 2002 to a level that will ensure that it remains below the three per cent limit under "normal" business cycle conditions. More precisely, the authorities plan to reduce the deficit in annual steps to 1.4 per cent in 2002. The debt-to-GDP ratio is scheduled to decline from 64.3 per cent in 1997 to the Maastricht reference value of 60 per cent. The debt reduction will be helped by privatisations and credit sales.

On the spending side, planned consolidation virtually comes to a halt in that the projected increase in revenues between 1997 and 2002, totalling Sch 232.8 billion, will almost entirely be utilised for spending increases (Sch 228.1 billion additional spending). This largely results from the planned expansion of social spending. This, in turn, reflects the fact that the government defines the goals of reducing unemployment and maintaining social cohesion as focal points of its economic policy agenda for the period under consideration. Indeed, in reforming the family support system the government attached a high weight to equity considerations, thereby increasing the degree of income re-distribution within the system at the expense of higher budgetary obligations.

Combined with additional employment-related outlays in the context of the NAP, spending increases and foregone revenues due to new social programmes (including the reform of the family benefit system and labour-market expenditures) will account for around Sch 15 billion or ½ per cent of GDP in 2000 compared to 1998. Given that social spending programmes are hard to reverse once introduced, the programmes are likely to constitute a lasting budgetary burden for later years.

Cyclical vulnerability

Based on the OECD's projection for the deficit in 2000, which is 0.2 per cent of GDP higher than the projection of the government, the fiscal consolidation path set out in the Stability Programme might not achieve the targeted deficit reduction to 1.4 per cent by 2002. But even if this target could be met under current growth projections,[15] it appears not ambitious enough to prevent breaching the 3 per cent deficit limit in the event of adverse economic developments. Based on estimates of the sensitivity of the general government deficit with respect to economic shocks, the OECD has simulated the probability of breaching the 3 per cent deficit limit over a pre-specified period of time under the assumption that public spending and tax parameters remain unchanged.[16] Generally, the likelihood of exceeding the 3 per cent limit increases with both the size of the deficit at the beginning of the period and the length of the period considered, since over a longer time span there is an increased probability of a sequence of unfavourable events hitting the economy. The results indicate that for a one-year horizon a deficit-to-GDP ratio of somewhat less than 2 per cent would suffice to keep within the 3 per cent deficit limit at a confidence level of 90 per cent. However, in order to avoid breaching the threshold with 90 per cent confidence over a five year period, the initial deficit would have to be smaller than 1 per cent.

Figure 8 shows the evolution of the general government deficit until 2002 under the assumption that fiscal policy contributes, *ceteris paribus*, to lowering the deficit in accordance with the steps specified in the Stability Programme, and taking into consideration the occurrence of economic shocks. In the absence of such shocks the deficit is assumed to decline to 1.4 per cent of GDP in 2002 (solid line). But adverse developments in the economic environment can push up the deficit above the targeted path. In the scenarios considered, attention is confined to deficit outcomes which occur with a probability of 10 per cent according to the OECD's estimates. Starting from the 1998 deficit of 2.1 per cent of GDP, there is a probability of 10 per cent that adverse shocks will drive up the deficit to 3 per cent of GDP or more already within one year, and to 3.3 per cent or more by 2002, even if fiscal policy contributes to reducing the deficit by about 20 basis points annually. Similarly, if in 1999 the deficit comes in at 2 per cent, as projected by

Figure 8. **Evolution of the deficit under adverse economic conditions**
Per cent of GDP

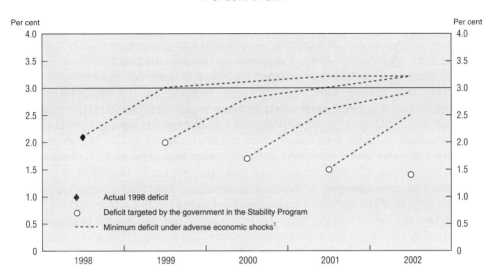

1. The shocks considered comprise real supply shocks, real private demand shocks and nominal shocks. With an estimated probability of 10% the deficit would be at least as high as the dashed lines indicate. For each starting year, it is assumed that the government continues to reduce the structural deficit by the amount specified in its Stability Program, despite the deterioration of the actual deficit.
Source: Ministry of Finance, Stability Program for the years 1998 to 2002; OECD.

the government, there is a probability of 10 per cent that it could be pushed upwards to 3.2 per cent or more by 2002 despite the government's current consolidation measures. From this perspective, the deficit targets of the Stability Programme cannot be considered sufficient to eliminate the risk, induced by a downturn in economic activity, of a breach of the 3 per cent limit which would require procyclical action.

Structural budget challenges

While the Maastricht constraints have undoubtedly helped to accelerate the consolidation process, corrective action would, in any case, have been needed to correct the surge in the budget deficit in the 1993 to 1995 period. This tendency for public spending and borrowing to deviate from a sustainable medium-term path was evidence of fundamental flaws in the budgetary control process.[17] An important feature of the recent retrenchment process has been the significant progress made towards better institutional control over public spending (discussed below), which should ensure that outturns are nearer to planned spending paths. But the recent shift in priorities towards higher social spending suggests that achieving the targets set out in the Stability Programme still depends on the eventual outcome with respect to the major public spending programmes. More particularly, it depends on the spending and revenue implications of recently-introduced or planned measures in the fields of pensions, health care and social reform, which are uncertain. In the past, the trend increase in social spending has been particularly dynamic in relation to overall general government outlays (Figure 9). Since 1960 both public health expenditure and pension insurance outlays grew more than twice as fast as GDP, though recently instituted reforms have managed to slow down this growth. The planned tax reform also poses a budgetary risk, not just with respect to the implied revenue responses to any changes in key tax parameters, but also to the bargaining process by which the various parties involved agree on the net reduction in the tax burden. The proposed cut is currently Sch 30 billion, equivalent to about 1 per cent of GDP in 2000 (including the tax relief from the family support package). The principal pressure points with respect to pensions, health spending and tax reforms are reviewed below.

Figure 9.   **Public health and pension-related outlays**
Index 1967 = 100

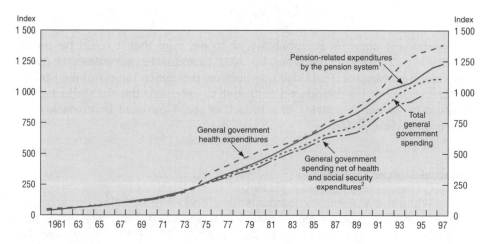

1.   Except civil servants *(Beamte)*.
2.   Total spending excluding health, social security pension and welfare expenditures.
Source: Government submission; OECD, *National Accounts*; OECD, *Health Data 98*.

Pressures on the pension system

In the longer term, budget consolidation needs to be seen against the background that pension outlays are set to increase, due to the interaction of unfavourable demographic developments and generous benefits. Prior to the November 1997 reform (described in the 1998 *Survey*), implied contribution rates (derived under the assumption of no transfers from the federal budget) were projected to rise from 30.2 per cent of the wage base in 1995 to 42.8 per cent in 2030, which would have implied rising pressure on federal transfers to the pension system. The pension reform has reduced the generosity of early retirement pensions and introduced a number of subsidised schemes for part-time work to encourage older workers to stay in the labour force. The obligation to pay social security contributions has been extended to all labour income, thereby bringing casual jobs into the pension system.

However, while the pension reform package represents progress in a number of areas, the legislated amendments will not resolve the fiscal pressure which an ageing population will create.[18] The statutory minimum age for early retirement (60 or 57 years for men and 55 years for women), remains exceptionally low in the OECD area and the discount for retiring early remains biased against staying employed. Generous transition arrangements are in force which could make the problem worse for some years. Eligibility conditions for early retirement in the old-age branch of the pension system have been tightened, but the take-up of invalidity pensions has increased (see Chapter III). Extending the contribution base to all labour income will improve the short-term financial position of the system, but the consequence could be pressures to obtain the minimum pension, especially from those with a work history of casual employment thereby generating substantial net costs in the longer term. The reform plan adopted in November 1997 recognised the need to pre-empt the long-term fiscal bias built into the pension systems, and mandated the introduction of an annual pension adjustment formula to take account of the evolution of life expectancy. However, introduction of the adjustment has been delayed without specifying a date for implementation: the pension increase was only small in 1998, and is likely to remain low in 1999 due to the slow growth of wages,[19] and under these conditions a demographic adjustment would have resulted in hardly any increase at all. Delaying the incorporation of a demographic component into the adjustment formula will inevitably increase the future fiscal burden implied by population ageing, with potentially adverse affect on labour costs.

Implementing reform in the health care system

As noted in previous OECD *Surveys* of Austria, spending pressures have been particularly marked in the health care system and introducing greater efficiency has become a matter of urgency. The government has responded by introducing cost-reducing measures in the 1996 and 1997 budgets, including measures to increase the revenues of the health funds and to bring hospital financing together under one institution for each federal state, which should help rationalise decisions. Since January 1997 hospitals are financed by nine separate Länder funds which, since all levels of government and the health funds are involved, subject the hospital system to a global budget constraint in each federal state. The costs of each individual hospital are reimbursed according to a scheme based on the diagnosis (*leistungsorientiertes Krankenanstaltenfinanzierungssystem*), similar to a fee for service, which replaced the previous per-diem reimbursement scheme. In the new scheme points are allocated to medical procedures based on performance-oriented diagnosis-related groups, and later reimbursed according to a valuation which, given the need to enforce the budget constraint, differs between Länder. Hospitals with either high levels of staffing or large investment in equipment receive additional compensation which also varies by Länder. Although information on the effectiveness of the reform measures is limited, there is evidence that they have helped to curb public outlays for the provision of health services (See the 1998 *Survey of Austria*).

Recent data confirm progress in containing costs in the hospital sector. The diagnostics-based reimbursement scheme reduces incentives for long hospital stays which were inherent in the old reimbursement system. The average length of stay in hospitals has continued to fall, with the decline in 1997 slightly exceeding the reduction in previous years. Overall costs in the hospital sector appear to be stabilising at a growth rate of around 2 per cent, although drawbacks are apparent, notably, an increase in the number of day admissions to hospitals suggesting that there could be some further shifting of treatment from the ambulatory to the hospital sector (Figure 10). Also, the transparency of service provision appears to have improved. The proportion of specific documentation of central diagnoses in hospitals increased from 70 per cent in 1996 to 79 per cent one year later. Further insights into more efficient hospital management are expected to arise from model projects established in 1998 covering issues such as admissions and discharge management, and co-operation between departments. The projects involve eleven hospitals and are scheduled to last for three years.

While progress in this field appears encouraging it should not distract policy makers from continuing reforms to remedy shortcomings in the health care system that have been identified in the last two *Surveys*. Different reimbursement rates across Länder and hospitals could nullify the benefits of moving to a diagnostic-based reimbursement system, since hospitals would be reimbursed effectively on the basis of costs. The next stage of reform should therefore be to standardise the criteria by which hospitals are remunerated, so as to reward institutions which make the most efficient use of resources. In addition, there is still a lack of integration between the stationary and ambulatory sectors. As has been argued in the 1997 *Survey*, improvement in this field requires that the

Figure 10. **Costs in the hospital sector**

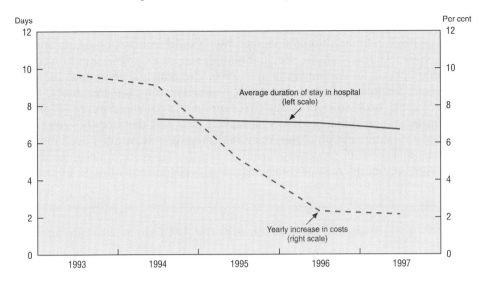

Source: Ministry of Labour, Health and Social Affairs.

ambulatory sector provides better access to a full range of services in one location. Setting up group practices should therefore be encouraged, and fees in the
ambulatory sector should be structured so as to give incentives for weekend
services and home visits. Duplication of tests could also be reduced and the
efficiency of care improved if practitioners were allowed to participate in their
patients' treatment in hospital.

Pressures for further tax reform

The 1998 *Survey* provided an in-depth analysis of the principal features of
the Austrian tax system and discussed policy issues involved in the current policy
debate. Following the important tax reforms of 1988 and 1993 and further changes
in recent years, the tax base has been widened and statutory income tax rates are
fairly standard by international comparison; marginal effective tax rates for investment and for savings have been brought down generally and the differences
between tax rates according to investment type, source of finance and type of
savings instrument have been much reduced. Nevertheless, despite this trend
towards "tax neutrality", pressures for further tax reform have arisen from a number of directions. Most fundamentally, the increased fiscal burden from
expanding social commitments has led to rising charges on labour with adverse

implications for incentives to expand employment. This has led to calls for tax measures which would reduce the relative price of labour. Also, claims have arisen in the political arena to address environmental concerns by raising resource taxes, with additional revenues being used to lower other tax burdens. With a view to further reform, the government set up a Commission to report on available options for implementation in 2000. The principal guidelines for reform comprised: fostering distributional equity, reducing labour-related taxes, fostering ecological taxation, increasing the simplicity and transparency of the tax system, securing revenue neutrality and taking into consideration the high degree of international integration of the Austrian economy. In November 1998 the Commission presented its proposals for reforming the tax system along these lines and a summary of the main recommendations is contained in Box 1. A number of

---

Box 1.   Proposals for tax reform by the Tax Reform Commission

Major areas for which reform is proposed are the following:

A.   Reduction of non-wage labour costs:

Various options are presented to finance a reduction in pay roll contributions of firms:

- Higher taxes on energy. With the tax base defined broadly, revenues would amount to between Sch 40 and 50 billion, depending on whether energy intensive enterprises would obtain rebates. They could be used to abolish the employers' contribution to the Family Equalisation Funds (*Familienlastenausgleichsfonds*). With the tax base defined narrowly, revenues would amount to Sch 8 billion. They could be used to abolish the employers' contribution to the residential construction support programme (*Wohnbauförderungsbeitrag*) which is run by the states.
- Higher real estate taxes (*Grundsteuern*) could be utilised to abolish the employers' contribution to the residential construction support programme (Sch 8 billion). Independently of reducing the tax burden on labour, a reform of the real estate tax system is seen as necessary since discrepancies in the valuation of real estate are considered to be unacceptable.
- Broadening the contribution base from pay roll to value added components. The reduction in the taxation of labour would also lead to an overall tax relief of labour intensive companies at the expense of capital intensive companies. The rebasing could be done for employers' contribution to the Family Equalisation Funds.

B.   Reform income taxation

- Revise the statutory income tariff rates such that existing hikes in marginal tax rates – in particular for low incomes – are smoothed out.
- A number of special income tax allowances could be abolished.

(continued on next page)

(continued)

C. Reform enterprise taxation

- Increase preferential tax treatment of outlays for both business research and apprenticeship training.
- Revise other features of business taxation such as profit assessment and conditions for company taxation on a consolidated basis.

D. Reform taxation of capital income

Reform the system along the following principles:

- As a rule, all capital income should be taxed according to uniform standards.
- Capital income from abroad should be subject to the same rules as domestic income.
- As a rule, the tax rate should be 25 per cent and would be a final tax (*i.e.* not simply a withholding tax).
- The present provision that capital gains from selling shares should be taxed only if the shares are sold within one year after their purchase should be dropped; the same principle should apply for real estate.

Higher tax receipts from the reform should preferably be used to reduce the income tax rates.

E. Reform inheritance and gift taxation

Reform the system along the following major lines:

- Simplify the system and increase its EU compatibility.
- Extend taxation to capture all wealth transfers and make taxation uniform across assets.
- Treat wealth transfers within families preferentially.
- Introduce special rebates for the assets of enterprises in case of a change in ownership.

Higher tax receipts from the reform should be used to reduce the tax burden on labour.

F. Reform taxation of private pensions

Create incentives for private pension provisions by reforming taxation along the following lines:

- Contributions to pension schemes and pension payments should be subject to the same tax rules, independently of the type of the scheme. Contributions to private pension schemes paid out of (already-taxed) wages could effectively be exempted from taxes via government bonuses (*Prämienmodell*).
- Contributions and capital accumulation should be exempted from taxation while returns should be taxed.

G. Revise the system of administrative fees

- Base charges for public services on transaction taxes for the purpose of making the system more simple and transparent.

Box 2.   **Tax reform measures announced by the coalition parties
on 23 March**

1.   Income and wage tax reductions

- Statutory tariff rates for wage and income taxes will be lowered, especially on low incomes.
  Tax relief: Sch 17 billion.
- Bonus payments for contributions to voluntary pension schemes.
- Tax concessions for voluntary payments made by companies to dismissed workers covered by a social plan (*Sozialplan*).

2.   Family and child allowances

Phased in two steps (1999 and 2000) family benefits and per child tax breaks are being increased.

Tax relief in 2000 compared with 1998: Sch 12 billion. This measure had already been announced in 1998.

3.   Business taxation

Several tax measures aim at fostering the attractiveness of Austria as a business location and at promoting employment.

- Tax concessions for research and development.
- Tax concessions for training apprentices (until 2002).
- Tax concessions for young entrepreneurs starting an enterprise.
- Abolition of inheritance and gift tax for most enterprises being passed to heirs.
- Tax concessions for capital participation in the film industry.
- Waiving of the mineral oil tax for the utilisation of environment-friendly fuel based on rape seed alcohol (*Rapsmethyläther*).
- Adjustment of turnover taxation in agriculture.
- Reduced taxation on profits equal to notional interest payments on equity capital.
- Abolition of the stock exchange turnover tax (*Börsenumsatzsteuer*), but an extension of the holding period to avoid capital gains tax from one to two years.

4.   Simplification and closing tax loopholes

Several measures aim at a simplification of tax rules and tax administration, in particular for small companies.

5.   Improving administration

A study will be commissioned scrutinising the cost effectiveness of administrative procedures.

---

proposals go in the direction of greater tax neutrality recommended by the 1998 *Survey* and should be implemented by the government, including the abolition of special income tax deductions; the unification of inheritance and gift taxation across assets; the unification of taxation across types of capital income; subjecting pension contributions and payments to the same taxing rules, and greater reliance on user charges.

The government coalition partners have subsequently determined the features of a further tax reform. The options for capital and environmental taxes are tightly constrained by the mobility of capital and international competition. A decision was made to exclude raising environmental taxes. Moreover, with the revenues of the real estate tax accruing to the communities and federal support for residential construction accruing to the Länder, changes in these fields would affect the inter-state fiscal equalisation system which has been fixed in negotiations between the federal government and the Länder until 2001. The coalition partners have therefore decided to exclude as policy options changes in these areas. As noted above, the coalition has agreed on a net tax relief volume of Sch 30 billion – including Sch 12 billion stemming from the reform of the family support scheme – which will accrue predominantly to labour (see Box 2). While reducing the tax burden is welcome, the extra budgetary strain will need to be met by reductions in public spending.

Improving public sector governance

The 1998 *Survey* recommended that a key priority for reducing the overall burden of taxation was a reappraisal of spending programmes. In particular, programmes with a regressive content (such as housing subsidies) would benefit from a more efficient targeting of social programmes since many benefits accrue to high-income families. In parallel, public sector efficiency needs to be improved, and in line with the government's policy programme, a number of measures to reform the public sector have been taken in the past few years. As part of the process of meeting the Maastricht criteria, public entities with commercial objectives have been "corporatised" by moving them from the general government to the public-enterprise sector, representing an opportunity to place their operation on a more efficient and commercial basis. Fundamental reforms have been undertaken with respect to the civil service, with moves to reform the pension system and to reconsider tenure and individual labour contracts. Steps have also been taken to clarify and to devolve competencies to the Länder and to establish a consultation mechanism to avoid costs being passed from one level of government to another.

Corporatising administrative units and privatisation

As mentioned above, the process of shifting business-oriented administrative units (whose revenues are derived by at least 50 per cent from market income) into the enterprise sector has continued at all levels of government, but appears to be particularly pronounced at the community level. An amendment to the budget accounting rules now requires corporatised entities to report their assets and liabilities and they are also required to produce evidence of proper management. While corporatising commercially-oriented administrative units may increase public sector efficiency, previous OECD *Surveys of Austria* have pointed to the risk that shifting public entities off-budget can jeopardise fiscal discipline in the public sector. This is especially the case where quasi-autonomous, non-government, entities receive government guarantees for their borrowing. In addition, there is the risk that such entities derive their profitability from being sheltered from market competition leading to a conflict of interest between the general economic responsibilities and the budgetary concerns of the state. Improving public sector efficiency will, therefore, require careful financial controls and an opening to market testing including competition from alternative providers.

As for the completion of the privatisation process, at present, the government's shares in *Telekom Austria*, the Post Office (*gelbe Post*) and the Post Bus (*Postbus*) are combined in a holding (*Post und Telekom Austria Aktiengesellschaft*, PTA). In October 1998 25 per cent of Telekom Austria was sold to STET/*Telecom Italia*. But intentions for further privatisations in the post and telecommunications area appear to be vague. A complete separation of the Post Office and the Post Bus would be necessary to prepare further privatisations to underpin improved competition and efficiency. Present legal conditions allow a privatisation of 49 per cent of the Postal Savings Bank (*Österreichische Postsparkasse*) without further legislative changes being required. While privatisation within this framework is planned for 2000, the ground for a complete privatisation needs to be prepared. After further placements in 1999, 59 per cent of Austrian Tobacco Works (ATW) is now in private hands.

Increasing the accountability of the public administration

Important steps have been taken to strengthen administrative control of the budget process. Since January 1997 each ministry within the federal administration has to present monthly budget reports outlining both the development of receipts and outlays and a comparison of targeted and actual outcomes, together with proposals for corrections. To facilitate performance reporting, in 1997 the government launched a project to develop effectiveness and efficiency indicators for the federal administration in which all departments participated. A set of performance indicators has since been developed. Fields in which various public sector activities are considered comprise, amongst others: school education and university training (both in co-operation with the OECD),[20] policing, national defence, tax enforcement, working conditions in transport, care of the disabled, consumer protection and protection of the environment. The government now aims at extending the coverage of administrative activities and improving the quality of the indicators. To collect data for benchmarking performance across countries, Austria also launched an EU-wide inquiry on performance indicators in the EU member states. The responses from this exercise were presented in November 1998 and are being utilised in follow-up projects at the EU level for developing international benchmarking indicators.

With respect to human resource management in the federal administration, some progress has been achieved. While in the past civil servants have regularly been granted tenure after a certain period (*Pragmatisierung*), this practice has now been given up. In addition, tenure is no longer a precondition for promotion to higher posts in the federal administration.

Improving federal fiscal relations

As has been noted in previous surveys, the devolution of costs to the federal government for projects which are decided by the Länder has created incentives for overspending. The federal, state and local governments have now agreed on a system which determines that for every legislative or regulatory measure the implied costs for other layers of government need to be assessed. Subject to certain thresholds, any government affected by net cost spillovers can demand negotiations on burden sharing in a consultation council comprising high level representatives of all three layers of government.[21] If the council does not arrive at a unanimous agreement about cost allocation, the government passing the legislation or regulation has to bear its full costs. Litigious cases would be dealt with by the Constitutional Court. Measures relating to EU provisions, taxation and the system of revenue sharing are exempted from this mechanism.

By making it more difficult to pass on costs to other governments, this framework should contribute to reducing the incentives for over-spending in the public sector. But given the low share of own revenues[22] the Länder will continue to rely heavily on federal co-financing of regional projects. To the extent federal co-financing is involved, the true costs of providing goods and services are not fully reflected in the Länder budgets and a tendency for over-spending could remain. Hence, further reforms of federal fiscal relations should follow, aiming at increasing the congruency between spending and financing for each government level.

The Stability and Growth Pact

A supplementary motivation for reforming federal fiscal relations derives from the requirements of the EU Stability and Growth Pact. Austria is obliged under the terms of the Pact to observe a general government deficit limit of 3 per cent of GDP and to accept sanctions including fines in the event of non-compliance (see Box 3). All layers of government agreed on binding domestic allocations of the Maastricht deficit limit. The arrangement stipulates maximum deficit allowances for the Bund of 2.7 per cent of GDP and for the Länder and communities of 0.3 per cent of GDP. It is proposed that penalties imposed by the EU for incurring an excessive deficit would be passed on to the government levels

---

Box 3. The Stability and Growth Pact

The Stability and Growth Pact clarifies the Maastricht Treaty's provision for dealing with "excessive deficits" and provides an institutional framework for its enforcement, in part through strengthened surveillance and co-ordination of economic policies *via* the annual review of national stability programmes. The Pact also calls on participants in the Economic and Monetary Union (EMU) and those countries with a derogation from initial participation in stage 3 of EMU – the actual introduction of a single monetary policy – to adopt budgetary balance (or even a surplus) as the medium-term objective.

The Pact considers a general government deficit above 3 per cent as excessive unless the European Union judges it to be temporary and there are special circumstances. Temporariness implies that, according to the projections of the Commission, the deficit would fall beneath the 3 per cent threshold in the following year. In the case of an excessive deficit, the Council will, on the recommendation of the Commission, propose a course of action for the country which should be followed by effective measures within four months. The Council will monitor the measures and if they are found to be inappropriate it will make further more detailed proposals, which will be published. If corrective measures have not been implemented within ten months, sanctions will be imposed. These would initially take the form of non-remunerated deposits, with a fixed component equal to 0.2 per cent of GDP and a variable component rising in line with the size of the excessive deficit. Such deposits are limited to a maximum of 0.5 per cent of GDP per year, but would accumulate each year until the excessive deficit is eliminated. Provided the excessive deficit is corrected within two years the deposits are returned to the country, otherwise the deposits will become non-refundable. In the event that the measures taken by a country are ineffective, the whole process will be restarted, but sanctions will be imposed within three months.

When a country is judged to be in recession, which is defined as an annual fall in real output (GDP) of at least 0.75 per cent, the Pact will be enforced in a differentiated manner. If economic output in a member country declines by 2 per cent or more – and provided the deficit is temporary – exemption from the procedure is granted automatically. In the event GDP falls by between 0.75 per cent and 2 per cent, exemption can be granted in special circumstances by the Council. The country would need to convince the Council that the economic decline was "exceptional" in terms of its abruptness or in relation to past experience.

---

* Sanctions do not apply to those countries with an opt-out or derogation from participation in stage 3 of EMU.

in accordance with their violation of the domestic deficit allocations. In cases of deficit over-runs due to natural catastrophes or other extraordinary circumstances, the allocation of the penalties would be re-negotiated.

Supplementing the Maastricht arrangement by a domestic stability pact could reinforce the process of fiscal consolidation. In particular, it could serve to eliminate any possible incentive for the Länder and communities to run excessive deficits at the expense of the Bund which would have to pay the fines imposed by the EU. But to be effective the system of domestic deficit allocation needs to be seen in conjunction with the system of inter-governmental revenue sharing. At present, the allocation of revenues is largely negotiated. Out of total revenues to be shared between the different levels of government certain subsidies and transfers to special funds (like the funds for family allowances) are deducted beforehand. The percentage of net tax revenues which will accrue to the Länder and communities are negotiated for classes of taxes and laid down in a federal law, which normally remains in force for four years. The more often revenue allocations are negotiated, the higher the risks are that deficit caps are not considered effectively binding which in turn would undermine consolidation efforts. Hence, rules for revenue sharing should be fixed on a long-term basis. For similar reasons, the deficit limits should not be negotiable, and exceptions from fixed penalty allocations in cases of deficit overruns should be clearly defined and confined to a minimum.[23] Also, the financial burdens implied by penalties should not be allowed to trigger burden sharing or equalising transfers from other governments.

III. Progress in structural reform

Introduction

Previous *Surveys* have recognised the Austrian labour market as being relatively well-performing. In particular, it exhibits a high aggregate wage flexibility and comparatively low level of unemployment, particularly among youths. There has, nevertheless, been a secular tendency for long-term unemployment to increase, and when seen in a longer-run perspective, employment growth has been only moderate. Unemployment has been held down by incentives to early retirement, which have made for a rather low labour force participation rate and relatively high non-employment among the older segment of the population. Recent *Surveys* have thus emphasised the need for faster employment growth *via* the further dismantling of regulations in labour and product markets which inhibit relative wage and work-time flexibility and by enhancing competition, enterprise creation and technological diffusion. The OECD recommendations have been given against the background of significant ongoing policy initiatives, which can be expected to improve the functioning of the labour and goods markets. Most recently, these have been drawn together and supplemented by new measures in the *National Action Plan for Employment* (NAP), which Austria submitted to the European Union in April 1998. This chapter reviews the policy measures which have been introduced since the last *Survey*, highlighting fields where the OECD would recommend further action in the context of the OECD *Jobs Strategy*. Issues relating to entrepreneurship are dealt with in more detail in Chapter IV.

Recent labour market developments

Recent labour market outcomes are in line with the established pattern in Austria in which a high degree of aggregate wage flexibility tends to lead to relatively stable employment over the business cycle. Average employment increased by almost 1 per cent in 1998, supported by GDP growth of some $3^{1}/_{4}$ per cent. Employment gains were around the EU average, while economic growth exceeded the average by around $^{1}/_{2}$ per cent. On the other hand, unemployment

Figure 11.   Labour-market indicators

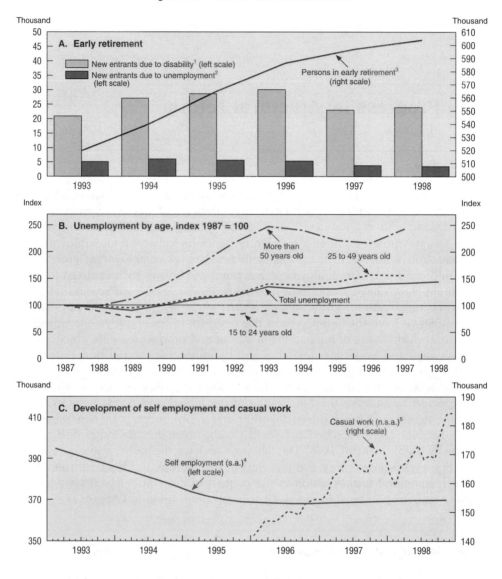

1.   Invalidity and reduced capability to work, excluding the self-employed.
2.   Excluding the self-employed.
3.   Here defined as early retirement in the old-age pension scheme and invalidity pensions.
4.   1998 quarterly data based on annual estimation.
5.   *Geringfügig Beschäftigte.*
Source: WIFO; Government submission; Arbeitsmarktservice Österreich (AMS).

increased marginally to 7.2 per cent (national definition), as labour force participation showed the usual tendency to rise with cyclical output gains. This process
was reinforced by measures contained in previous fiscal consolidation programmes, notably the curbing of special unemployment benefits for the elderly
(*Sonderunterstützung*) and the tightening of benefits for parental leave.[24] Labour
supply continues to be held down, however, by large inflows into early retirement, both in the old-age branch of the pension system and on account of
invalidity. Having declined in 1997, the inflow into early retirement – including
invalidity pensions – stabilised at a high level in 1998 (Figure 11).

Part-time employment has increased significantly in recent years, its
share in overall employment rising from around 11 per cent in 1996 to almost
13 per cent in March 1998.[25] Information from the micro-census indicates that this
development is broadly based, but is particularly pronounced in retail trade,
health and financial services.[26] In particular, the liberalisation of shop opening
hours in January 1997 contributed to the rise in part-time employment. Indeed,
the rapid increase in part-time employment accounted for the bulk of employment creation in 1998, absorbing most of the increase in female labour
supply.

Youth unemployment, which is traditionally low in Austria, declined significantly in 1998, while unemployment among the older age groups increased
further. In 1998, registered unemployment among youths aged 15 to 18 was
7.7 per cent lower than the year before, and in the 19 to 29 age group it declined
by almost 4 per cent. By contrast, unemployment rose by 7 per cent among the
persons aged between 50 and 54 years and by more than 28 per cent for people
aged 60 or more (Figure 11). To a large extent this development reflects adverse
movements in unemployment duration. The length of registered unemployment
spells declined for the 16 to 18 year age group, whereas it increased for those
aged 60 and above. Overall, the average duration of unemployment spells for
those still registered (*Vormerkdauer*) levelled off at 230 days and the number of
long-term unemployed (longer than one year) increased by ½ per cent.

Progress in structural reform

The framework for structural policy evolved during the course of 1998,
with the agreement between the government and the social partners on the
National Action Plan for Employment (NAP), which will be monitored by the Council of
Ministers of the European Union. The plan specifies concrete targets for the
increase of employment and for the decline in the unemployment rate up to 2002
and, reflecting the guidelines laid down by the EU, lays particular emphasis on
youth unemployment and equal opportunities (see Box 4). In terms of strategy, an
important role is assigned to active labour market measures for combating

Box 4. The National Action Plan for Employment

The Austrian government and the social partners agreed in April 1998 a "National Action Plan" to foster employment. The plan is based on four principal pillars which EU member governments have recognised at the EU's employment summit in Luxembourg in the autumn of 1997 to be central for securing high levels of employment. These are: fostering employability, entrepreneurship, adaptability and equal opportunities.

In line with the decision of the Council of Ministers of the EU, the government has specified a number of quantitative targets which it will seek to achieve by 2002:
- Expand employment by 100 000 persons (dependent employment in 1997: 3.06 million) and lower the unemployment rate to a level close to 3.5 per cent (unemployment rate in 1997: 4.5 per cent).*
- Halve the inflow into long-term unemployment of young people under the age of 25 and of adults.
- Ensure that 20 per cent of the unemployed participate in active measures preparing them for entry or re-entry into the labour market.

Major elements of the National Action Plan are:
- Fostering active labour market policies, in particular by redirecting funds from "passive" to "active measures".
- Fostering business start-ups by accelerating approval procedures and making available seed and risk capital.
- Developing the educational system by adapting vocational training curricula, increasing the supply of training places, developing the polytechnic institutions in tertiary education (Fachhochschulen), and fostering the co-operation between universities and polytechnic institutions with enterprises.
- Reducing seasonal unemployment through an improved distribution of work time.
- Reforming the tax and contribution system in an employment friendly way, in particular by reducing the tax burden on labour.
- Combating illegal employment and black market activity.
- Fostering research and innovation for the purpose of increasing the level of employment.
- Utilising potential demand for social, health and environmental services to increase employment and to encourage the development of manufacturing-related services.
- Providing additional care facilities for children and the elderly for the purpose of fostering the compatibility of employment and family.
- Fostering supply conditions by increasing public infrastructure investment.

---

* Employment as defined by the Central Statistical Office. The unemployment rate is the standardised Eurostat definition and not the definition used by the OECD for Austria. For a description of the differences see OECD *Economic Survey of Austria*, 1997, Annex II.

unemployment, in particular among younger age groups, but the Plan also identifies a range of other elements considered to be important for raising the employment capacity of the Austrian economy – notably tax reform, the development of the education system, simplifying administrative requirements for setting up enterprises, and export promotion. Many of the structural policy measures embodied in the Plan actually predate it, so that the NAP should be seen as incorporating aspects of existing policy approaches. The published plan lists a wide range of areas in which action is to be taken, and a framework for monitoring and sequencing the implementation of the NAP has been installed. New EU guidelines are now being introduced to broaden the NAP to deal with the problem which most affects Austria, namely unemployment among older workers and the need to raise the employment rate in this group of the labour force.

Increasing wage and labour cost flexibility

Previous *Surveys* have noted that the social partners have taken steps to increase wage and working time flexibility at the plant level and the wage round for 1999 was differentiated with wage increases of between 2½ and 3½ per cent. In the metal and electrical engineering industry the collective agreement of 1997/98 allowed companies to deviate under certain conditions from the generally-agreed wage rate. In a survey conducted in January 1998 by the metal workers union, 6 per cent of firms, covering about 22 per cent of employees in that sector, responded that they used this opening clause.[27] According to another estimate, in the autumn of 1998 one third of the firms made use of the provision. The results indicate that there is a substantial demand for more flexible arrangements. Consequently, the opening clause has been renewed in the latest collective agreement in the metal and electrical engineering sector.

The need for flexible arrangements also extends to the regional level. In the crafts and trades branch, collective tariff agreements are bargained for each sector between the federal crafts or trades association and the union, but to become effective they require approval by a majority of the Länder employers associations (*Innungen*). Several regional employers associations in the crafts and trades area have refused to accept federally-negotiated agreements. The 1998 collective wage agreement in the metal crafts sector has even been rejected by some Länder associations. In addition, some industrial employers have reportedly sought to be redefined from industry to crafts or trades so as to fall under a more favourable wage agreement. In response, the unions have proposed to reorganise the system of employers' representation in the crafts and trades area such that collective agreements concluded on the federal level are automatically binding on the regional level. But such a system would reduce wage flexibility unless accompanied by wider opening clauses than at present.

Increasing working-time flexibility

With respect to working-time flexibility, progress has been made but it appears to be uneven and working time regulations remain complex.[28] In tourism a new collective agreement, affecting some 160 000 employees, has widened the scope both for shift work over the week and for averaging the calculation base for overtime premia. On the other hand, the Austrian Trade Unions Federation (Österreichischer Gewerkschaftsbund) has demanded sector-by-sector cuts in the average weekly working time to 35 hours and has called for raising the costs of overtime work. In the wage round for the retail sector, which commenced in October 1998, the trade union has demanded a reduction in the average working time from 38.5 hours to 35 hours for some 400 000 employees and the introduction of overtime premia for work time in excess of 38½ hours. Lowering the threshold for overtime premia would be at variance with demands for more working time flexibility.

Policy measures designed to subsidise shared and part-time employment, which were contained in the 1997 pension reform package,[29] could act to reinforce the trend towards more part-time employment, although there are no indications as yet that these schemes are effective. Up to June 1998 the "solidarity premia model" (Solidaritätsprämienmodell), which provides financial incentives for reducing the working time of older employees in favour of new hiring, had been implemented by only two enterprises. Part-time employment is set to gain importance in the public sector where the government has eased the relevant regulations.

Following strong growth in 1996 and in the opening months of 1997, the expansion of casual employment (geringfügige Beschäftigung) at first declined but then grew strongly through 1998 (Figure 11). In the past, casual employment and work commissioned by firms from self-employed (Werkverträge) were largely exempted from the obligation to pay social security contributions, but since the end of 1997 employers are subject to contributions. While the levy has lessened the rise in marginal tax rates previously associated with the transition from casual to part-time employment, it has simultaneously raised labour costs in this more flexible end of the labour market. The fact that such employment has expanded at the same time is due to a changing employment structure, particularly in the retail sector following the liberalisation of opening hours. Employees can opt to become part of the social security system by making their own contributions at a reduced rate. Very few employees have made use of this option, suggesting that they were already covered either through the contributions of a spouse, the family, or from other employment.

Reducing the distortions arising from unemployment insurance and related benefits

Unemployment benefits

As noted in the 1998 *Survey*, incentives to work were increased from January 1998 with the implementation of a new regulation allowing benefits to continue to be paid, at a reduced rate, if a person on benefits accepts a part-time job to less than seventeen days per month. While no direct data are available on the part-time employment of benefit recipients, the rapid growth of part-time employment in the past year might indicate that the programme has been quite successful.

Out of concern to protect the social security contribution base and in line with commitments in the NAP, the government has tabled a law designed to step up controls to prevent black-market activity. Recipients of unemployment benefit who are found working in the black market will be sanctioned as though they had worked illegally for the entire month except where they can prove the opposite. To make the identification of black-market work easier, employers now need to register their employees on the first working day rather than the third day as in the past. Disputes have arisen, however, about the appropriate definition of "work" and whether "help for neighbours" should be included. The debate shows the practical difficulty in implementing additional legal controls. This has since been resolved.

Early retirement

Previous *Surveys* have identified generous early retirement conditions as distorting incentives for efficient wage bargaining and this, in combination with higher social charges to finance retirement, represents a major impediment for higher labour utilisation in Austria. In the public sector, early retirements have recently declined substantially. The share of new retirees younger than 60 dropped from two-thirds in 1995 to two-fifths in 1997. This was accompanied by a dramatic decline in the number of retiring civil servants, such retirements in 1997 amounting to less than one third of the peak in 1995. While this development is related to previous hiring policies in the public sector, it also reflects the introduction of discounts for early retirement pensions for civil servants (prior to age 60).

In the general pension system, as noted in Chapter II, eligibility conditions for early retirement (*i.e.* before the age of 65 for men and 60 for women) were tightened as part of the 1996 fiscal consolidation package. Inflows into old-age early retirement have subsequently declined, by 22 per cent in 1997, and by a further 3 per cent in 1998. However, despite sharpened eligibility conditions for early retirement on account of reduced capability to work, which became effective in January 1998, new retirements in this group have decreased by only 0.3 per cent. Simultaneously, there has been an increase in the take-up of invalidity pensions by 7.7 per cent, which has almost offset in absolute terms the reduction of early retirement inflows in the old-age branch. This supports the view that different channels into early retirement serve as substitutes for each other if access to such schemes is not tightened across the board[30] (Figure 11). Overall, in 1998 old-age early retirement pensions and invalidity pensions combined continued to account for four-fifths of all new pensions granted (excluding survivor's pensions), the same as in 1997. Following measures to restrain access to pensions on account of reduced capability to work by raising the period of sickness to 20 weeks, no further tightening of eligibility conditions for other programmes is planned until 2000.

Active labour market measures

In order to achieve the quantitative targets set out in the *National Action Plan* (Box 4), the government intends to expand active labour-market measures (ALMPs) significantly. To combat long-term unemployment, the government aims to offer placements in active labour market schemes to all unemployed who are at risk of becoming long-term unemployed and have undergone counselling to evaluate their eligibility for such schemes. This will apply two to four months before the person becomes unemployed for more than six or twelve months. Financial support will also be given to enterprises and institutions for the purpose of fostering the qualification and integration of the unemployed. Unemployed who are found eligible to participate in active labour market schemes can also obtain financial aid covering expenses for training, commuting and child minding. Funds of the Labour Office (*Arbeitsmarktservice*) devoted to active labour market measures and associated income support increased by 5.4 per cent in 1998 and are set to rise by another 14.9 per cent in 1999 with financing to be covered in part by a related reduction in expenditures on passive programmes. An assessment of the government's new ALMPs will have to await implementation in the coming months since experience in other countries indicates that the effectiveness of such programmes depends largely on programme design.

In the context of the NAP, the federal authorities and the Länder have agreed to increase employment in occupations providing social and health services. The Länder and the communities will extend their facilities for providing such services, while the federal government will contribute to financing both employment and training. In addition, it will also co-finance regional infrastructure investments for the development of structurally-weak regions and the associated outlays for employment, provided such projects contribute to net employment creation. These proposals need to be made consistent with health sector reform and with the desire to improve public sector efficiency. With respect to infrastructure investment, project selection procedures are at present highly variable with most ministries relying on a number of boards and commissions which include the social partners; in some of these, project planning is not well developed. In order to avoid the danger of waste with the new scheme, it will be crucial to reinforce planning procedures, but proposals in this area are not yet known. Empirical studies generally fail to find any across-the-board relationship between public investment and growth, while more specific studies which focus on types of investment or on particular regions find impacts that vary from very strong and positive to zero or even negative.

Improving skills, entrepreneurial dynamism and competition

The OECD *Jobs Strategy* recognises the importance of a balanced approach to ensure that labour market equilibrium is achieved in conjunction with social welfare objectives. For this to be the case, labour force skills need to be fully exploited and developed, technology effectively utilised and entrepreneurial dynamism promoted. At the same time, financial markets and goods markets need to be made competitive and efficient. In this way the marginal product of labour would rise to help validate existing wage rates thereby lowering adjustment costs. The requirements for promoting entrepreneurship are dealt with in Chapter IV, the remainder of this chapter focusing on more specific issues concerning skill formation, capital markets and product market competition.

Improving skills and technological know-how

As noted in the 1998 *Survey*, adapting the apprenticeship curricula to new demands is a crucial element in modernising Austria's hitherto successful dual vocational training system. The process of creating new curricula continued in 1998 and a first evaluation indicates that applications for training in new fields appear to be significant. For the year as a whole, 12 per cent of newly-concluded apprenticeship contracts were in areas which have been newly established since September 1997.

Despite this progress, apprenticeship places available in 1998 fell short of applications, as in previous years. This caused the government considerable concern, all the more so in view of the emphasis given to dealing with youth unemployment in the NAP. In response, the government and the social partners agreed on further measures to support the vocational training system, extending previous *ad hoc* measures adopted as part of the 1997 policy package.[31] To lower the costs of training for employers, a tax credit has been introduced for firms during the first year of an apprenticeship and the employers' contribution to social security has been waived. These measures have been incorporated formally into the NAP. No further measures to ease legal restrictions on the employment of apprentices have been included in the programme.[32]

Even though the school and apprenticeship systems are highly effective at providing education and training to a high proportion of the population, a relatively low, but still significant number of youths still leave school without sufficient qualifications and slip through the safety net of the training system. For such youths a "pre-apprenticeship" curriculum has been established – at present for a probationary period – to smooth the transition to regular apprenticeship training. Pre-apprenticeship courses spread the regular first-year vocational training over a period of up to two years. Participants are directed to pre-apprenticeship training by the Labour Office (Arbeitsmarktservice). In addition, a special "rescue network" has been set up to create training places for up to 4 000 youths who did not find training places. The programme, the duration of which is limited to two years beginning in the autumn of 1998, provides financial assistance to institutions (which usually do not provide apprenticeship places) for organising ten-month vocational courses. These courses are required to convey the knowledge of a first-year regular apprenticeship, with 60 per cent of the training being practical. The high weight given to practical skills is a positive feature of this programme, but emergency programmes designed to fill the gap between applications and offers could face problems of matching skills to needs, which will require careful monitoring.

With respect to schooling and tertiary education, attention has focused on increasing the occupational relevance of the curricula and introducing business training into non-business oriented studies, but progress in this difficult area has been slow and uneven. A five-year development plan (beginning in 2000) is being prepared for the polytechnic institutions (Fachhochschulen), which have specialised in providing applied tertiary training. In addition, a major aim of the reform measures, incorporated in the 1997 University Act, is to link the university curricula more closely to the needs of the labour market. Implementation of the university reform has been held back by a delay in finalising a number of out-standing regulations and ordnances.

The level of R&D expenditures is relatively low in Austria, and in combi-nation with evident deficiencies in the innovation system (reviewed in more detail in Chapter IV) has led the government to develop a "Technology Offensive". The programme was outlined in last year's Survey and has been incorporated into the NAP. Progress has been made in implementing programmes designed to establish and support research networks ("Centres of Competency", Kompetenzzentren), which involve research institutions and enterprises.[33] However, the past year has also been marked by major conflicts about the institutional structure to support science policy in the government. The establishment of "Centres of Competency" constitutes a key element of the "Technology Offensive". Two ministries are involved in developing their own support schemes. In addition to the scheme of the Ministry for Science and Transport, which focuses on the establishment of competence centres at relevant universities, the Ministry of Economic Affairs has developed two further schemes, one industry-based and the other subject-based. The objective of the industry scheme is the development of centres grouped around competence cores in industry. The other scheme is defined as a "network of several complementary competence nodes" under specific topics like biomass, aeronautical technology and forestry products.

Developing financial markets

As far as the financial market is concerned, the most significant developments have concerned the creation of the euro area which should lead to the creation of deeper and more liquid capital markets. Domestically, the most important step has been the reorganisation of the Vienna Stock Exchange (*Wiener Börse*); the stock exchange has opted for a close co-operation with the Frankfurt Stock Exchange. In this context, the exchange will adopt the German trading system (*Xetra*) (implementation is planned for the second half of 1999), and membership in one of the two bourses will be mutually recognised, such that members of the Frankfurt Stock Exchange will have automatic access to listings at the Vienna Stock Exchange and *vice versa*. These measures should go a considerable way to increasing the depth of the Austrian equity capital market. In a similar vein, the market segments of the stock exchange have been redesigned. In particular, a new segment, the "Austrian Growth Market" (AGM), has been established for the purpose of facilitating the funding of medium-sized companies. It replaces another special board (FIT), which was not successful in attracting companies and capital. The AGM is a potentially important innovation in that it requires companies to report in accordance with international accounting standards and accompanies each newly-listed firm with a market maker, thereby attempting to improve market liquidity. The development of venture capital institutions is discussed more fully in Chapter IV.

A new take-over law, *inter alia*, protecting the interests of minority shareholders, became effective at the beginning of 1999, and is likely to have a positive impact on the propensity of financial investors, both domestic and foreign, to engage in stock market financing.

Increasing product market competition

Deregulating the telecommunications sector

With respect to the opening of the telecommunications market, competition has developed rapidly in both the fixed network and the mobile sector. Following the new telecommunications law, which came into force in August 1997, key regulations under the responsibility of the new regulatory authority (*Telekom Control Kommission* and *Telekom Control* GMBH) were established during 1998. The commission has defined fees for interconnection, and the mode by which customers can choose different networks has been simplified. In the process, 50 licences for fixed network (voice telephony and leased lines) were granted in 1998 and another three licences in mobile telecommunications. The regulatory framework should provide a base for alternative network operators to compete, provided the authorities monitor the scope for downward revisions of the interconnection fees and implements adjustments as expeditiously as possible. Interconnection fees account for a high percentage of the current costs of providers of telecommunication services and their level is crucial to the fostering of market access. Unbundling at the local levels of the network might be required to support competition. Reducing telecommunications costs is particularly important for the competitiveness of Austrian industry in view of the fact that telephone charges are significantly higher than the OECD average.[34]

The electricity sector

In accordance with the EU directive, a new law for the electricity sector (Elektrizitätswirtschafts-und-organisationsgesetz, ELWOG) came into force in February 1999, designed to partially open the sector to competition from this date onwards. The law determines that networks are obliged to grant access to generators and eligible customers. In the past, a major impediment for a regulatory structure favouring competition has been the concern to preserve the interests of the federal states over their utilities (see OECD Survey 1998). In the current debate three issues are of particular importance: creating non-discriminatory conditions for network access, setting up a tariff system for the utilisation of the transmission network which does not disadvantage new competitors, and solving the problem of stranded costs.[35]

Regarding network access, the government now supports the "regulated third party access" model, which appears more appropriate for opening the energy market than the "single buyer" model.[36] The new legislation stipulates that the regulator (the Ministry of Economic Affairs) can deny network access in order to secure electricity supply from generators which need to fulfil public service obligations (gemeinwirtschaftliche Verpflichtung). These obligations are fulfilled by environmentally-friendly and resource-saving combined generation/central heating generators or for systems based on renewable resources, provided these generators are operated in an efficient, "business-like" manner. These provisions carry a risk that established energy providers might be sheltered at the expense of new competitors unless precise benchmarks are set down for assessing whether generators are operated in a business-like manner. Such ground-rules will be difficult to implement in the absence of competitive market forces. In a similar vein, the law specifies preferences for existing contractual arrangements or contracts which follow-up existing arrangements. Securing the benefits of lower energy prices will require that granting market access be based on the principle of non-discrimination with exceptions confined to a minimum.

Tariffs for the utilisation of the transmission and distribution network, which maintains its monopoly position, have been determined by the Ministry of Economic Affairs. Given the complex federal structure of the system, tariffs vary by region and by voltage level on the basis of the full costs of maintaining, running and extending the network (*i.e.* historical investments), including discounts in the range of 3.5 to 10 per cent for prospective productivity gains. Scattered public ownership of both networks and generators makes the unbundling of the grids from other parts of the electricity supply chain difficult to put into effect, especially with respect to the efficient pricing of network utilisation, which is a crucial condition for competition among suppliers for eligible customers. Transmission fees are currently substantially higher than in other European countries which will create a barrier to market entry for new energy suppliers, thereby allowing established utilities to skim monopoly rents at the expense of their customers.

An issue which had to be resolved, with a potentially significant impact on the openness of the market, concerned the allocation of the costs associated with Austria's high voltage network. The Minister of Economic Affairs favoured using the entire electricity consumption in Austria as a base for allocating these costs (gross method), but the Länder generators (*Landesgesellschaften*) and the communities (*Kommunalgesellschaften*), which are to a certain degree independent from the high voltage grid, argued that the costs should be allocated to the grid's customers only(net method). The latter method would have implied higher prices for the utilisation of the high voltage grid than the former and would have constituted a barrier to entry for new generators. In January 1999, a compromise system was adopted – incorporating the gross and the net methods to 40 and 60 per cent respectively – subject to self-generated electricity (and some other sources) being excluded from the computation base.

Competition policy

Competition policy issues have become more important recently with allegations about cartels in a number of branches of the building industry, an EU inquiry into an alleged interest-rate cartel among banks, and controversy about how major mergers in the retailing sector should be handled and by whom: by the Austrian authorities or by the EC. These developments have raised questions about whether the present framework is effective in protecting competition, and whether it can assume an adequate subsidiarity role in the context of EU competition law. The current system is based on a cartel court (*Kartellgericht*) which acts on the recommendations of the social partners (represented by the Federal Chamber of Labour and the Federal Business Chamber) while the Ministry of Economic Affairs (Department for Competition) represents the State before the court. Cartels are not prohibited and the cartel court does not as a rule have the right to initiate actions independently. Although fines can be substantial, they have been applied only seldom.[37] The system is potentially subject to conflicts of interest on the part of the social partners and is vulnerable to political pressure. These dangers have been highlighted in the past year.

During 1998, there was a planned take-over of a major Austrian food chain by another company that fell, because of its large size, into the domain of the European competition authorities. In the context of requesting a partial referral of this case to the Austrian cartel court, important negotiations were held between the social partners and the Ministry about the conditions which might attach to the merger. Both parties to the merger and their competitors were and are members of the Business Chamber, which made it difficult to treat the issue objectively in the cartel court, due to potential conflicts of interest. Eventually an agreement was reached between the Minister of Economic Affairs and the firm planning the take-over. To restrict market power in the distribution sector, the arrangement would have set a ceiling for the market share of the new company after the merger (slightly lower than what the merged firms would have had), and also included employment and training obligations. Although this agreement was never put into effect – the EU indicated its objections to the proposed agreement and a formal request for its referral to the Austrian competition authorities was, as a consequence, not made – it illustrates certain problems. Bargains of this type run the risk of being sensitive to pressures by the interested parties which can undermine competition enforcement. Indeed, in the case under consideration the firm planning the take-over threatened to reduce its orders in Austria if the merger were prohibited. Similarly, there is the risk that enforcement of competition law may be compromised by encouraging concessions by the negotiating firms which are not related to competition issues or which involve sub-optimal remedies.[38] Another set of deficiencies became apparent in the case of the building industry. After discovering a building cartel, the City of Vienna placed some firms on a black list for public tenders. This provoked protests from the employees affected placing the representatives of labour in a conflict of interest. In this sense, the credibility of competition enforcement depends on the extent to which it is independent of the social partners and the government. The government has been planning to review the competition law for some time and a draft law has recently been sent to Parliament which will, inter alia, make Austrian law more compatible with EU regulations and allow the court to initiate actions. However, it stops short of creating an independent competition authority.

Overview and scope for further action

The structural reform process in Austria continues to be broadly based, covering not only the labour market but also the education system and product markets. An overview is shown in Box 5, together with the original Jobs Strategy proposals and recommendations for further action.

Box 5.   **Implementing the** OECD Jobs Strategy
– an overview of progress

Since the last review a number of policy measures in the spirit of the OECD Jobs Strategy have been implemented but progress has been mixed. This summary reviews progress since the Jobs Strategy recommendations were made for Austria in 1997

Job strategy proposal	Action taken since 1997	OECD assessment/recommendations
I. Increase wage and labour cost flexibility		
• Encourage wage differentiation, greater plant-level bargaining and opening clauses	Greater flexibility agreed by the important metal sector. Changed wage profile for white-collar workers.	Encourage the next step toward genuine opening clauses within the collective bargaining framework.
• Facilitate the employment of older workers and reduce incentives for early retirement	Subsidies introduced for employment of older workers and fines for dismissals. Relaxation of conditions for part-time pensions.	Encourage wage negotiations which seek to take account of the special situation of older workers. Make unemployment benefits more closely follow market wages.
II. Increase working-time flexibility and ease employment security provisions		
• Reform regulations underpinning inflexible working practices	Law governing hours of work liberalised allowing more flexible organisation of working time for industries taking advantage of this (*e.g.* metal).	Review effects of regulations and, when necessary, open possibilities for flexible agreements.
• Liberalise terms for renewing fixed-term contracts	Restrictions reviewed and assessed to require no action.	Keep situation under review.
• Facilitate part-time and casual work	Extension of obligation for employers to pay social security contributions extended to self-employment and to casual jobs. Benefits given to employees for working-time reductions which are associated with hirings of unemployed. Restrictions for part-time employment	Review the introduction of social security contributions for casual jobs and self-employment with a view to supporting the transition from unemployment to employment. Liberalise restrictions on working time by occupation.

(continued on next page)

(*continued*)

	in the public sector eased.	
• Reform dismissal protection	Existing regulations reviewed and assessed to require no action.	Keep situation under review.

III. Reduce the distortions arising from unemployment insurance and related benefits

• Reduce the incentives for early retirement	Early retirement on account of unemployment restricted. Additional restrictions will be phased in mainly from 2000. Incentives for early retirement pensions reduced.	Consider further means to curb early retirement in the short term and strengthen longer-term measures (stricter eligibility criteria, higher actuarial discounts for pension benefits).
• Reduce unemployment benefits to seasonal workers in the tourist industry	No action.	Proceed with reforms.
• Reduce disincentives to take up work in social assistance programmes and develop in-work benefits	Unemployment benefits and assistance are now gradually decreased for temporary employment, rather than immediately withdrawn.	To lower marginal effective tax rates at lower income levels, further examine possibilities to raise earnings disregards while simultaneously lowering benefits rapidly as people approach full-time employment. Develop in-work benefits in the context of greater wage differentiation.
• Give greater emphasis to active measures and less to passive measures	Subsidies now paid to employers for employing those on unemployment assistance. For those on leave, a subsidy is paid if an unemployed is hired to fill the job or if training is taken up. Subsidies introduced for working time reductions which lead to hirings of unemployed.	Monitor to see whether the restriction to take on unemployed is administratively feasible and that leave is not abused and becomes costly for the economy.
	Financial aid to firms and the unemployed for training and integrating the unemployed is being	Focus the measures narrowly on problem group. Evaluate effectiveness of schemes.

(*continued on next page*)

(continued)

	expanded. Employment in social and health occupations to be promoted. Subsidies for employment associated with regional infrastructure investment.	Embed support for social and health sector employment in wider reforms which encourage efficiency and sound finance. Ensure efficient infrastructure investment.

IV.   Improve labour force skills

• Preserve and restore the attractiveness of the dual vocational training system, clarify its relationship to higher education	Curricula for some apprenticeships revised and new occupations introduced. Health insurance contributions for apprentices waived and work hours of apprentices liberalised. Industrial subsidies and procurement contracts to be linked to training. Tax break granted and injury insurance contribution waived for companies taking on apprentices. Financial assistance to institutions organising additional vocational training.	Continue to revise vocational training curricula and occupations. Avoid attaching subsidies and procurement to training. In new support programmes for youths who have not found apprenticeships, ensure that market forces are important in determining the type of training to be offered.
• Shorten and reform higher education and focus it on more occupational-oriented studies. Extend role of new higher level schools (Polytechnics)	New university law which allows for shorter study periods.	Shorten higher education and make it more occupationally oriented. Continue with reform of universities. Examine potential for moving some study fields to the new institutes of higher education.

V.   Enhance creation and diffusion of technological know-how

• Foster venture capital markets and reduce regulatory barriers	Government has encouraged stock exchange to merge with options and futures markets. Vienna exchange now to link with Frankfurt. New single regulator for financial markets. Voluntary take-over code	Tax reform to lower the high effective rate of tax on equity. Widen the potential for investment funds to take equity in enterprises. Focus public financial support programmes on complementing private

(continued on next page)

(*continued*)

	introduced. Programmes to encourage venture capital and business angels.	funding.
• Stimulate the diffusion of technology	Technology package being implemented which seeks to raise level of R&D. Clusters to be promoted in basic research and employment of scientists in industry subsidised. Competence centres being established.	Continue with basic reforms of the university and tertiary sector to encourage greater integration with the economy and increased productivity of research funding.

VI. Support an entrepreneurial climate

• Facilitate the establishment of new enterprises	Regulations governing commencement of a trade liberalised (*Gewerbeordnung*). New restrictions on opening large-surface shopping centres to protect local shops.	Continue to examine regulatory impediments and improve procedures especially at Länder level. Further liberalisation of trades law and of hours of trade.
	Legislation tabled to shorten approval times for plants.	Implement new approval law and continue to streamline regulatory requirements.
• Reform bankruptcy law to facilitate reorganisation	Reform to bankruptcy law, changing governance incentives and powers of individual creditors. Reorganisation procedures established with financial sanctions for directors if bankruptcy follows.	Monitor effects of reorganisation law. Consider extending protection to companies under restructuring. Improve discharge procedures allowing faster re-entry to business life of an entrepreneur.
• Planning approvals needs to be simplified	Approval procedures simplified and in some states down to three months.	Monitor the effectiveness of the new procedures and continue reform.

VII. Increasing product market competition

• Encourage competition in the net-work sectors	Telecommunications and electricity liberalisation laws in force. Regulated third party access rather than single buyer	Continue implementing the telecommunications law to promote effective competition. Ensure that

(*continued on next page*)

(continued)		
	adopted for electricity sector.	access to electricity network is granted in a non-discriminatory way. Set network fees in both sectors at competitive levels.
• Barriers to entry in the provision of local services to be lifted and public and private suppliers placed on an equal basis	No major changes although a number of entities have been taken off budget.	Abolish preferential treatment of public suppliers. Introduce greater market testing
• Pursue privatisation	Creditanstalt privatised and steps made to lower state role in another bank. Tobacco monopoly privatised	Step up privatisation and prepare Telekom for sale. Review restrictions on privatisation in the electricity industry
• Establish independent competition authority	Agreement on limited reforms.	Review requirements of EU law and complete reforms, including new independent competition office

In the context of the overall strategy embedded in the NAP, some caution is needed with respect to the employment and unemployment targets adopted by the government (see Box 4). Targets may be valuable where they induce structural policy adjustments to achieve them, and the discipline that setting objectives can impart is evident in the attempt to link these to concrete measures. However, evidence in other OECD economies suggests that too heavy an emphasis on numerical targeting could induce a bias towards active labour market and employment-creation measures at the expense of structural reform, and this should be avoided. While a shift from passive to active labour-market measures appears appropriate in the Austrian case, over-utilisation of such measures would introduce new inefficiencies into the labour market which may be costly to remedy at a later stage. In any case, numerical targets should not give the misleading impression that the government holds the main responsibility for labour markets outcomes, when its principal role, with the social partners, is one of setting the conditions for private sector job-creation.

Active labour-market measures play an important role in the government's new employment strategy. Indeed, reallocating funds in favour of active measures can be useful to the extent that this improves the adaptability of the unemployed to labour market conditions. Experience in other countries has shown, however, that for such measures to be effective they need to be tightly targeted.[39] Also, there is a risk that private sector entrepreneurial activity is crowded out by public work programmes. Plans to increase employment in the health and social sectors may conflict with the need to improve efficiency and to secure long-term financing. A structurally-sound health sector might well be an important source of job creation in the future, but directly stimulating employment could give wrong signals and set false incentives. To minimise these risks, it is very important that the effectiveness of active labour market and job creation measures be constantly evaluated.

The Austrian labour market exhibits a comparatively low level of unemployment and high aggregate wage flexibility. But there has, nevertheless, been a secular tendency for long-term unemployment to increase, and when viewed over time the level of employment has only risen moderately. While part-time employment has increased significantly, helped by a liberalisation in shop opening hours, progress with respect to increasing wage-cost and working-time flexibility has been uneven. Advances in this field will largely depend on the social partners. To improve labour market outcomes, greater flexibility in labour costs and working time should be encouraged at the corporate level. More specifically:

i) Reports suggest that opposition to federally agreed wage bargains in the manufacturing/non-industrial sector (Gewerbe) is significant and reinforce the case for assigning a larger role to collectively-agreed opening clauses. While retaining general framework agreements at the sectoral level, such clauses would introduce a certain degree of flexibility at the firm and regional level. Recent experience with collective framework agreements in some sectors has shown that such arrangements are compatible with social partnership.

ii) Lowering the threshold for over-time premia through legislation could have an uncertain impact on employment, but would be at variance with demands for more working time flexibility and should be avoided.

iii) The effectiveness of subsidised part-time employment schemes needs to be monitored to facilitate revisions if necessary.

iv) Legal restrictions on working time by occupation remain complex and regulations of this type should be liberalised.

v) Scope could still remain for unemployment benefits and social assistance schemes to be revised such that marginal effective tax rates are lowered at the transition to (legal) employment. This needs to be investigated further and could be achieved by phasing out benefits over a longer income range than is presently the case.

With respect to pensions, the demographic pressure on contribution rates, and hence on labour costs, has been only temporarily alleviated by the recent reforms. Further measures would appear necessary to tighten eligibility conditions across all types of early retirement if inflows into early retirement are to be curbed, while incorporation of a demographic component into the pension adjustment formula is needed to prevent an insupportable increase of the future fiscal burden implied by population ageing. The option to develop additional private pension provisions needs to be looked at more closely, and this requires an appraisal of the incentives given by the tax system with respect to personal and occupational pensions (see Box 1).

The modernisation of the curricula of the apprenticeship system appears to have been well-received. On the other hand, incentive measures designed to stimulate short-run demand for apprentices may not introduce trainees into occupations with the most promising longer-run prospects. Such schemes need to be carefully monitored to minimise the risks. To build up the attractiveness of the education system, further adaptation of skill profiles and a widening of apprenticeship curricula will be required. Since the polytechnic institutions (*Fachhochschulen*) are recognised as providing valuable occupationally-oriented tertiary education, it would be worthwhile extending the range of studies offered by them to other fields, notably social and life sciences. In this context, further efforts should be made to shorten university studies and to transfer to the polytechnics studies hitherto the preserve of the university sector.

Considerable progress has been made in a key area affecting entrepreneurial dynamism, by introducing shorter and more efficient approval procedures for setting up new enterprises and installing plant and equipment. Recommendations in this area are dealt with more fully in Chapter IV.

The restructuring of the Vienna Stock Exchange should help to improve enterprise financing, but further steps to widen the capital market should follow. Legislating take-over conditions has been important in this respect. Support for enterprises *via* subsidised credit should not be considered a substitute for improving the functioning of the capital markets and the further development of venture capital markets (Chapter IV).

The regulatory framework for product market competition has improved, but there are a number of areas where more needs to be done to ensure a genuine competitive environment:

　　　　i) Significant progress has also been made in establishing the legal conditions for opening the markets for telecommunications and electricity to competition. However, the pricing of network interconnection should not be allowed to create new barriers to effective market entry and to competition. Efficient pricing should be supported in both sectors by a privatisation policy which could be an effective device for unbundling the network operation from users. In the electricity sector care needs to be taken that market access is granted in a non-discriminatory way.

ii) Recent developments in construction, retailing and banking underline the need to establish an independent competition authority for the purpose of initiating investigations and actions in support of a strengthened competition law.

iii) Discriminatory restrictions in the trades law for setting up shopping centres should be reconsidered (Chapter IV).

Overall, the past few years has seen a number of important structural-policy developments, as Austria has adapted rather well to the new competitive conditions imposed by EU membership. The agenda for action – both legislative and by agreement of the social partners – has been wide, and the impact is already to be seen in improvements in the functioning of the labour and goods markets. The general thrust has been to increase the flexibility of both labour costs and working-time flexibility, while also making progress towards a regulatory environment based on greater competition, enterprise creation and technology diffusion. Nevertheless, the analysis above suggests that progress has been uneven and there remain important lacunae in the reform process. There are thus still important challenges to be faced.

IV. Promoting entrepreneurship

The OECD *Jobs Strategy* included a general recommendation that OECD countries needed to strengthen their entrepreneurial climate. Entrepreneurship, as the dynamic process of identifying economic opportunities and investing human and physical capital to create wealth, is central to the functioning of market economies and crucial to job creation. In recognition of this, major structural changes have been occurring in the Austrian economy, through which the former corporatist, state-sponsored approach to growth is being replaced by one based on private initiative. The 1997 *Jobs Strategy* review of Austria made a number of broad recommendations for building on the progress made in this direction and the government's National Action Plan for Employment (NAP) has proposed a number of areas for further policy initiatives. The objective of this chapter is to assess the current state of entrepreneurship in Austria, to identify the factors which might still be retarding or misdirecting entrepreneurial activity, and to review the policy options for enhancing Austrian performance in this area. Following a general discussion of the entrepreneurial climate, the first section reviews a range of widely used indicators of entrepreneurial activity, covering business start-ups, their survival and growth and the innovative activity with which entrepreneurial initiative is widely associated. It concludes that the extent of entrepreneurial activity, while widening in recent years, needs strengthening. The second section focuses on the factors which are likely to have affected entrepreneurship and which may be amenable to policy intervention, such as product market deregulation and the operation of financial markets. The final section presents the OECD recommendations for further policy action.

The scale of entrepreneurial activity in Austria

Entrepreneurship needs to be regarded broadly, since it can embrace the actions of new and well-established companies, both foreign and domestic, as well as the behaviour of individuals including the self-employed. Also, it is a process which clearly covers all economic activity and is not just confined to high-technology industries or particular business functions (*i.e.* marketing, internal organisation and distribution are also covered). Some companies and individuals in business may be characterised by significant entrepreneurial activity and capacities while others will be more reactive and adaptive. In view of the breadth and essentially qualitative character of the concept, no precise measurement of entrepreneurship is available, making it essential to review a range of indicators. Two types of indicators are usually considered. The first group focuses on the process of founding new enterprises, how some of them grow and how the unsuccessful ones disappear. Also important is the growth and vitality of existing firms. Start-up and survival rate statistics are indicators often used to examine this aspect of entrepreneurship. Other indicators focus on the self-employed and on the situation in small businesses where ownership and control are usually tightly linked, but the implicit reference point to an individual owner/entrepreneur needs to be handled with care. A second group of indicators focus on entrepreneurship as involving innovation and innovative behaviour. One such indicator is the number of patents but this is very imperfect: there are many examples of firms in one country patenting an idea only to see actual application by enterprises in other countries. However measured, precise international comparisons of entrepreneurship are difficult to make, and this general caveat needs to be kept in mind with respect to any conclusions drawn below.

Business creation, survival and growth

Background: the entrepreneurial climate

Despite a long period of rapid post-war growth, Austria has not always been a particularly favourable environment for entrepreneurial activity: even though there has always been a large number of private enterprises, the degree of corporatism was high up to the end of the 1980s, with many large firms in state ownership. Managerial positions in these firms were frequently allocated according to party affiliation, so that entrepreneurial business activity was second best to a political career.[40] Access to many business activities was tightly controlled by associations with legal status, and some individuals with a strong entrepreneurial inclination probably sought their opportunities abroad.[41]

With the changing structure of the economy, the potential importance of entrepreneurship has changed since the beginning of the 1990s. A substantial share of formerly state-owned enterprises have been privatised, the number of state-owned industrial firms having declined from 139 in 1988 to 79 in 1995. For banks the corresponding numbers are 72 and 43 respectively. Privatisation has resulted in a significant decrease in the size and importance of the public sector in the economy while at the same time contributing to improving its structure (Figure 12). Direct political influence over economic activity is now limited to public entities (such as some banks) and utilities, and even here appointments might now be based less on political affiliation than in the past.[42] At the same

Figure 12.   **The changing structure of the public sector**
Value added at current prices[1]

1988: 319.3 billion of Schillings; share of GDP:[1] 22.4

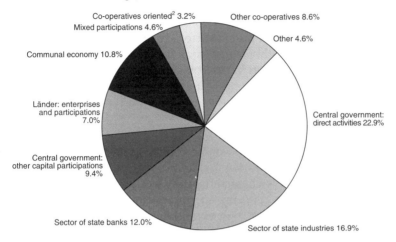

Co-operatives oriented[2] 3.2%   Other co-operatives 8.6%
Mixed participations 4.6%
Other 4.6%
Communal economy 10.8%

Länder: enterprises
and participations
7.0%
Central government:
direct activities 22.9%

Central government:
other capital participations
9.4%

Sector of state banks 12.0%
Sector of state industries 16.9%

1995: 360.3 billion of Schillings; share of GDP:[1] 16.8

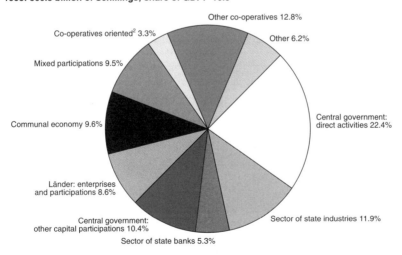

Other co-operatives 12.8%
Co-operatives oriented[2] 3.3%
Other 6.2%
Mixed participations 9.5%

Communal economy 9.6%
Central government:
direct activities 22.4%

Länder: enterprises
and participations 8.6%

Central government:
other capital participations 10.4%
Sector of state industries 11.9%
Sector of state banks 5.3%

1.   Excluding VAT.
2.   Au service de la communauté.
Source: WIFO.

time, the business sector is undergoing a far-reaching transformation as a result of admission to the EU in 1995: foreign direct investment has surged and is continuing at high levels, trade with the EU area has also expanded rapidly, and the single market has sharpened the competitive environment and reduced regulatory barriers to economic activity.

At the same time, public attitudes to enterprise have also been changing. Up to the 1990s the reliance on public sector job creation was such that entrepreneurship was not linked with income and employment growth in the public perception, but this has changed in the course of the 1990s; whereas in 1988 only a third of surveyed respondents saw a need for more self-employed business people, by 1998 a slight majority of those interviewed indicated such a need.[43]

Enterprise birth and death rates

Although internationally-comparable data on birth and survival rates for businesses are lacking – and national statistics are poor –, the balance of evidence suggests that Austria is characterised by low enterprise birth rates and by high survival rates.[44] The two concepts and the overall growth rate of the economy are closely related so that information about two statistics allows inference about the third. Even making allowance for differing conceptual systems, the survival rate in Austria appears to be internationally high (Table 9) especially over a five-year horizon. GDP growth was about average so that the business birth rate has

Table 9. **Firm survival rates**

Per cent

	After three years	After five years	Average growth of GDP 1990-1997
Austria	**83**	**72**	**2.3**
Denmark	69	58	2.5
Finland	63	55	0.9
France	62	48	1.5
Germany	70	63	2.4
Ireland	70	57	6.7
Italy	66	54	1.3
Netherlands	74	. .	2.7
Norway	68	53	3.7
Portugal	56	47	2.5
Spain	70	. .	2.1
Sweden	70	59	0.9
United Kingdom	62	47	1.8
United States	60	50	2.3

Source: European Observatory Annual Report 1995 and NFIB Small Business Primer. For Austria H. Wanzenböck, 1998.

been probably lower than in other countries, and anecdotal evidence points to a similar conclusion.

Although the enterprise birth rate has been lower than in other countries, new business creation has accelerated significantly. The most detailed study conducted to date indicates a 50 to 70 per cent rise in the number of start-ups in comparison with 1990: by one set of estimates,[45] the number of start-ups rose from 8 300 in 1990 (excluding take-overs of existing enterprises) to 14 200 in 1997, to which must be added around 4 000 businesses covering free professions and genuine self-employed.[46]

Increasing start-up activity is also reflected in an increase in the number of self-employed: after reaching a low point of 6.2 per cent of the non agricultural labour force, the ratio has now risen to some 8.2 per cent. There is also evidence that attitudes are changing: for those taking the masters qualification for trades, 70 per cent now wish to start their own business, in comparison with a ratio of around 60 per cent in the early 1990s.[47] Self-employment is, however, an ambiguous indicator of entrepreneurial qualities because the proportion of self-employment tends to fall internationally as GDP per head rises[48] – and, indeed, once the high level of GDP is taken into account, Austrian performance appears to be less of an anomaly than simple ratios would suggest (Figure 13). Nevertheless, attention is often drawn to the somewhat low ratio of self-employed to total employment in comparison with other EU countries (Figure 13, panel B).

Start-up activity is highly concentrated in the crafts/trades sector and in retailing. In relation to employment, the highest intensity is in retailing and construction while the lowest is in manufacturing. The latter characteristic probably reflects the small size of start-ups relative to the average size of existing enterprises and the higher level of investment needed to open an enterprise.[49] Sectors with high start-up rates – such as retailing – are also characterised by high exit rates. In comparison with Germany, there was a higher percentage of start-ups in retailing but fewer in services (Table 10).[50]

A great deal of public attention is devoted to start-up activity in high-technology fields, since there is evidence that new enterprises are an important transmission mechanism whereby new technologies and products are introduced and diffused throughout the economy. In both the manufacturing and service sectors every fifth start-up can be classified as in the high-technology area[51] although a greater number of high tech start-ups occur in the service sector. From the viewpoint of overall start-up activity, however, the proportion of high-technology in total start-ups (2 per cent) is not high and, on the basis of a comparable study, lower than in Germany.[52] This may be because the proportion of manufacturing start-ups is relatively low.

With respect to survival rates, three quarters of companies set up in 1990 were still in the possession of their original owners or their successors five years

Figure 13. **Self employment in an international perspective**[1]

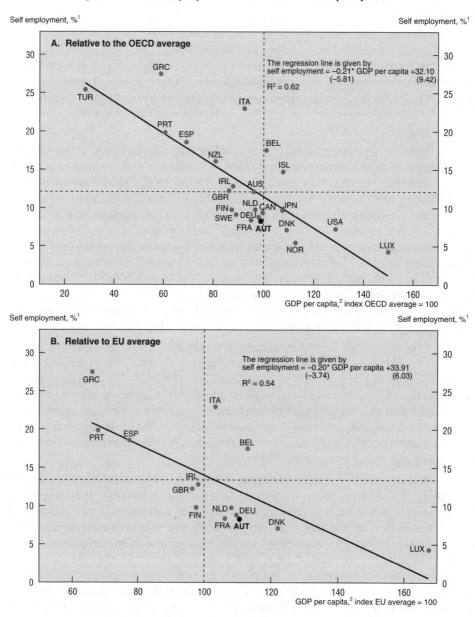

1. In 1996. Non-agricultural self employment as a per cent of total non-agricultural employment.
2. GDP per head, indices using current PPPs.
Source: OECD, *National Accounts*; OECD, *Labour Force Statistics*.

Table 10. **Sectoral incidence of start-up activity**

Per cent of total

Sector	Austria	Western Germany
Manufacturing	11.7	10.7
Construction	12.9	11.4
Retailing	37.7	33.2
Transport and communications	5.1	5.3
Services, banking and insurance	32.1	39.6
Other	0.7	. .
Total number of start-ups (1990-1994)	58 011	n.a.

Source: "Das Neugründungsgeschehen in Österreich", ZEW, 1998.

later although as in other countries the third year of operation is critical. Where they do disappear, as in other countries many companies are simply closed. Actual bankruptcy affects only a minority: 5 per cent in the Austrian sample cited above whereas 18 per cent of the start-ups were closed. One of the reasons for the relatively high survival rate is the large number of start ups by skilled craftsmen (M*eister*) who exhibit low failure rates. A factor behind this could be the rather long qualification period and the greater market and administrative knowledge on the part of the individual. Bankruptcy and firm closures affect firms other than new start-ups and over the past few years the number of bankruptcies have been high.

The regional dimension

Entrepreneurial activity as measured by business start-ups varies significantly between the federal states.[53] Part of the explanation is related to the sectoral composition of activity, since most new start-ups are in the area of retailing and services and these tend to be concentrated in urban areas. High-technology start-ups in manufacturing do not tend to be concentrated in an "urban incubator" setting as is frequently hypothesised, but there is some evidence that start-up activity in technology-related services (*e.g.* computing) is concentrated in urban areas. After allowing for factors such as urbanisation, sectoral structure and population, marked regional differences in this aspect of entrepreneurial activity remain with Vorarlberg (which is in the west of the country on the Swiss border) exhibiting particularly high rates as does Vienna.[54]

An important aspect of regional policy has been the development of technology parks. There are now some 30 centres among all the federal states, with approximately 800 enterprises employing some 6 000 workers. The presence of such centres has not been associated with a higher incidence of new start-ups in the regions where they are located. This surprising result could be due to the fact that the centres have often been established in depressed areas and that not enough time has elapsed for positive effects to become apparent (the study covered 1994). But it could also indicate that where technology parks are established for reasons of regional policy, spill-over effects might be limited due to reduced synergy and economies of scale.

Enterprise growth

As in many other countries, economic growth is probably driven by a comparatively small number of fast growing firms – some of which are long established – with the bulk of new firms remaining small. Only 13 per cent of new firms have more than three employees, while after five years of operation the average size of enterprise is only 3.5 persons including the entrepreneur. But some grow rapidly: evidence from a panel of technology-based new start-ups, which were supported by government programmes, indicates that some experience quite high growth rates, especially the subsidiaries of existing enterprises (Table 11).[55] However, the study did not permit a comparison to be made with the performance of existing enterprises, some of which are also growing rapidly: of the fastest-growing 500 firms in Europe,[56] 17 are Austrian which, given the size of the economy, is a relatively high number. Between 1992 and 1997 such firms grew by some 15 per cent annually and over this five-year period their employment grew by 8.6 per cent annually.[57] This is high in comparison with the European average. The firms were spread across several sectors, including building and tourism. Take-overs were important accounting for 45 per cent of turnover growth so that the net employment effect would have been smaller. Expansion by such firms was generally based on competitive pricing, an emphasis on human capital formation and a high rate of innovation.

Table 11. **Changing size distribution of new high-technology firms**[1]

Percentage of enterprises

Number of employees	New enterprises			New subsidiaries of existing enterprise		
	First year	Third year	Fifth year	First year	Third year	Fifth year
Under 5	86.8	45.7	30.7	46.7	28.6	22.7
5 to 9	9.9	36.0	27.5	30.0	17.9	4.5
10 to 19	1.4	14.0	24.8	0	21.4	13.6
20 to 49	1.4	2.2	13.1	13.3	14.3	31.8
50 and over	0.5	2.2	3.9	10.0	17.9	27.3

1. Based on a survey of enterprises supported by the government research fund (FFF) over the years 1984-1996.
Source: C. Lettmayr *et al.,* "Der Beitrag dynamischer Unternehmen zur Beschäftigungsentwicklung", *Wirtschaftspolitscheblätter,* 5, 1997.

New enterprises contributed significantly to gross job creation although net employment growth has probably been confined to a small number of new and existing enterprises. In the period 1990-1994, new start-ups created about 340 000 jobs (gross), or around 12 per cent of employment in 1991, according to one estimate.[58] This corresponds to an annual rate of gross job gains from openings of around 3 per cent which is about average for the OECD in this period.[59] The problem with such calculations is that they fail to take into account possible substitution effects whereby new start-ups would simply displace existing employment. The sectoral evidence available, nevertheless, suggests that new start-ups are sometimes associated with significant positive net employment effects.[60] Although the role of new firms in employment creation is important and these are overwhelmingly small it does not imply that employment growth is attributable to SMEs. Over the 1990-1998 period, the share of employment in small and medium-sized enterprises increased, although a more detailed analysis reveals considerable heterogeneity (Table 12): the growth of employment in plants with more than 500 workers has practically stagnated, although a certain a number of large enterprises have grown rapidly (*e.g.* in the 500 to 1 000 category).

Table 12.   **Employment growth by size of enterprise**

Employees per enterprise (excluding owner)	Number of enterprises		Total employment			Share 1998 in per cent
	January 1990	January 1998	January 1990	January 1998	Employment growth 1990/98	
1	89 807	96 752	89 807	96 752	7.7	3.9
2	32 465	35 277	64 930	70 554	8.7	2.8
3	21 149	22 796	63 447	68 388	7.8	2.7
4	14 300	15 424	57 200	61 696	7.9	2.5
5	10 470	11 246	52 350	56 230	7.4	2.3
6 - 9	24 156	24 334	165 910	175 845	6.0	7.0
10 - 14	12 043	12 711	140 768	148 660	5.6	6.0
15 - 19	5 766	6 309	96 718	105 757	9.3	4.2
20 - 29	5 771	6 015	137 544	142 907	3.9	5.7
30 - 49	4 525	4 878	171 577	184 338	7.4	7.4
50 - 99	3 278	3 621	226 046	248 064	9.7	9.9
100 - 199	1 770	1 834	244 212	255 471	4.6	10.2
200 -299	576	587	138 487	143 453	3.6	5.8
300 -499	402	440	151 256	166 227	9.9	6.7
500 -999	257	280	175 178	185 927	6.1	7.5
>1 000	165	149	391 386	384 306	−1.8	15.4
Total	226 900	242 653	2 366 816	2 494 575	5.4	100.0
1 - 99	223 730	239 363	1 266 297	1 359 191	7.3	54.5
100 - 499	2 748	2 861	533 955	565 151	5.8	22.7
>500	422	429	566 564	570 233	0.6	22.9
Total	226 900	242 653	2 366 816	2 494 575	5.4	100.0

Source: Main Association of Austrian Social Security institutions, aggregated and calculated by the Austrian Economic Chamber, 1998.

However, since employment growth in SMEs might also be the result of larger firms downsizing or breaking up, it cannot be concluded on the basis of Table 12 that SMEs were the main creators of jobs.

Innovation

Entrepreneurship is reflected in the ability to adapt to new situations and to seize and match new market and technological opportunities, and from this perspective, the performance of some Austrian enterprises, both domestic firms and subsidiaries of foreign companies, must be viewed positively: the extension of trade and investment into eastern and central Europe has been remarkable,[61] as has the ability to integrate rapidly into the EU which can be seen from the high growth rate of exports to the EU countries. This activity is not confined to large enterprises: a number of small-to-medium-sized enterprises report that a high percentage of turnover comes from exports and that they feel themselves well equipped to compete in foreign markets.[62] Indeed, several medium-sized companies are in the process of becoming small multinational firms (see Box 6). Austrian enterprises were, however, slow in establishing themselves in south-east Asia during the period of rapid growth.

On the other hand, international surveys show that although Austria is rated highly as a business location, the features which are found attractive do not relate to the ability to innovate. Rather than the entrepreneurial climate, the factor cited most favourably is the supply of well-trained and skilled workers (top managers were also regarded highly). The other positive factor referred to

---

Box 6. Examples of Austrian entrepreneurship

The success of Austrian-based companies and entrepreneurs is frequently overlooked. For example, AVL List of Graz is the largest privately-owned engine development company in the world with 25 subsidiaries and 15 engineering offices around the globe. Moreover, it has successfully branched into medical technologies. It has also probably been influential in the decision by companies such as BMW and Daimler-Chrysler to concentrate activities around Graz, which has developed as a cluster for auto technology. Topcall, an information technology group is quoted on the Easdaq and has been one of the top performing shares in Europe. Other companies which are well known abroad include Wolford in the fashion area. Although Austria is not the home to large multinationals on the order of companies such as Ikea, Philips or Nokia, a number of firms are developing into small multinationals which are significant in their own market niche. An example is VA Stahl which was privatised in 1995 although the government still controls a significant minority stake. The company – together with the closely associated VA Tech – have been active in acquiring stakes in foreign companies in speciality steels and in steel technology.

is the general quality of life. Patent protection (which is important for entrepreneurial activity) was given high marks. Factors ranked least favourably included telecommunications costs, access to risk capital, ability to adjust and desire to reform, the international standard of research institutions, and the public acceptance of new technology. In comparison to the standards set by the respondents for an innovative (and entrepreneurial) location, important deficiencies are thus apparent (Figure 14).

Figure 14.   **Assessment of the innovation system in Austria**[1]

Scale from high to low

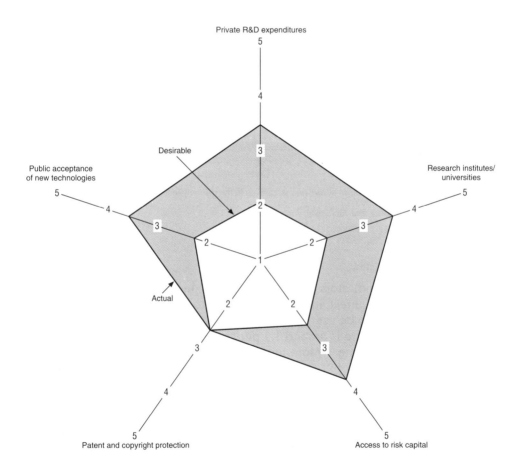

1.   The shaded area denotes the innovation gap between judgments about actual system and the assessment of what is desirable. The assessments are scaling from 1 (very high) to 5 (very low).
Source: G. Hutschenreiter *et al.*, Österreichs Innovationssystem im internationalen Vergleich, WIFO *Monatsberichte*, 7, 1998.

Figure 15. **Level and structure of R&D expenditures in the OECD area**[1]
Per cent of GDP

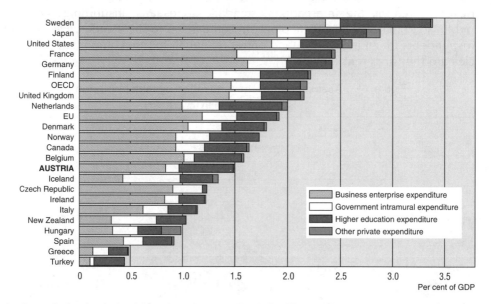

1. Due to the fact that the breakdown shown here according to the different sectors is not available for Austria after 1993, the graph refers to 1993.
Source: OECD, *Main Science and Technology Indicators.*

Technology indicators point to moderate levels of innovative activity, although with foreign direct investment (and technology transfer) increasingly important care needs to be used in interpreting national indicators. Research and development expenditure is around 1.5 per cent of GDP and is low for a country with a high level of income.[63] More importantly, Austria is in the bottom third of OECD countries in terms of R&D expenditures in the business sector (Figure 15). However, a broader definition of innovation expenditures including patents and other costs as well as R&D, reveals a much better relative performance, with innovation expenditures around 5 per cent of industry turnover. With respect to indicators of output, the number of patents issued to residents (the inventiveness coefficient) is also relatively low for a high income industrial country and those patents which have been issued are concentrated in the building industry (Table 13). Perhaps as a result, the level of high-technology products in industrial exports is only about half as high in Austria than in either the OECD area or the EU. On the other hand, there appears to have been a significant acceleration

Table 13. **Inventiveness coefficient**

Resident patent applications per 10 000 population

	Average 1981-96
Switzerland	5.34
Germany	4.95
Sweden	4.40
Australia	4.31
Finland	3.88
United Kingdom	3.42
United States	3.29
New Zealand	3.04
Austria	**2.84**
Norway	2.22
Denmark	2.19
France	2.18
Ireland	2.00
Netherlands	1.48
Italy [1]	1.34
Canada	0.90
Belgium	0.89
Spain	0.51
Portugal	0.09
Mexico [1]	0.06

1.   Average over the period 1992-96.
Source: OECD, *Main Science and Technology Indicators* 1998, Paris.

recently in the diffusion of new technologies related to information technologies and robots[64] and the rapid increase of FDI since 1995 might involve substantial technology transfer which is not yet fully apparent in the indicators.

In some circles innovation is not necessarily viewed as positive for employment but there is evidence that firms which are innovative also have a high growth rate of employment. Using a number of proxies for innovative activity related to the use of information technology, one study[65] classified around half its panel sample as not innovative, a quarter as weakly innovative and 8 per cent as strongly so. Innovative firms were found to generally exhibit employment growth rates much above the branch average, although there is some variability in performance which is to be expected.

Factors affecting the entrepreneurial climate

Although entrepreneurial activity, as manifested in new start-ups, growth, and innovation, is strongly influenced by cultural factors which are poorly understood, institutions and framework conditions are also important and are more amenable to change through policy interventions. This section first reviews the perceived barriers to entrepreneurial activity and attitudes to risk before considering the role of specific framework conditions such as product market competition, regulation, financial markets and government support policies.

Perceived barriers to establishment and growth

Start-up firms and the aspiring self-employed face a number of (real or perceived) barriers. Most frequently mentioned are finance and administrative problems, followed by difficulties in having qualifications approved under the trades law (*Gewerbeordnung*) (Figure 16). Closer investigation reveals that finance is

Figure 16. **Barriers to self employment**
Responses in per cent of total[1]

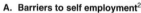

A. Barriers to self employment[2]

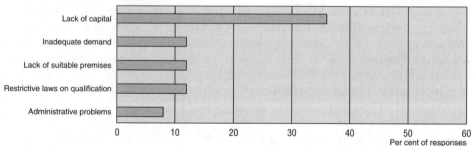

B. Absolute importance of barriers[3]

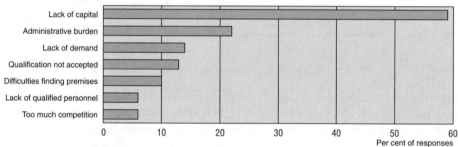

1. Of respondents citing the item as a barrier.
2. Respondents were allowed to choose more than one barrier.
3. Respondents were allowed to choose only one barrier.
Source: Institut für Gewerbe- und Handwerksforschung, 1996.

regarded as the most important barrier, followed by the tax burden and administrative impediments (Figure 16, panel B).[66] One third of survey respondents see finance as the key issue while 12 per cent regard problems with the trades law or business premises as critical (Figure 17). (If problems arise with premises or with the trades law they are regarded as critical, otherwise they are not regarded as a problem at all.) However, the above list often represent restraining factors rather than absolute barriers and several surveys suggest that only in exceptional cases do they prevent a seriously intended new enterprise from setting up business.

With respect to growth, established enterprises report a number of perceived constraints to business expansion which, taken as a whole, are significant in comparison with other European countries (Figure 18). Foremost among these is a lack of finance, followed by regulatory barriers and taxes (Table 14). These factors are also regarded as important in the shorter run, for which the lack of qualified and managerial staff are also regarded as important. Fast-growing firms do not see finance as a barrier, but the lack of management capacity was listed as a major constraint. In terms of framework conditions, which are relevant for policy formation, indirect wage costs, lack of labour resources (quality and quantity), bureaucratic barriers and inflexible working time arrangements all come into play.

Figure 17. **Perceived importance of barriers to self employment**
1 = very important, 2 = important, 3 = small, 4 = very small

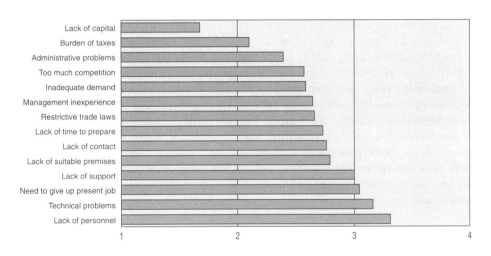

Source: Institut für Gewerbe- und Handwerksforschung, 1996.

Figure 18. **Main long-term constraints on business expansion**
Per cent of reponses[1]

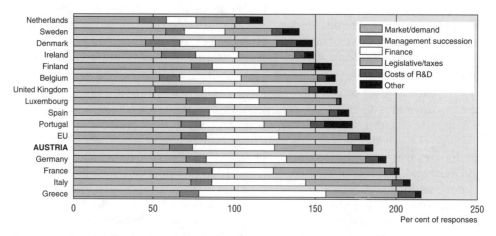

1. Sum of responses, given as percentage of respondents. Respondents were allowed to choose more than one
    constraint.
Source: Grant Thornton International Business Strategies Ltd, 1997.

The barriers to entrepreneurship noted above are often perceived ones and the implications in terms of policy are not always evident. Investigations in the area rely on the results of sample surveys but there are major difficulties with these and they must be interpreted with care: the surveys seek to clarify the constraints and motivations of either potential or actual entrepreneurs but the identification of either group is problematical. While indicators which focus on the entrepreneurial climate, in the form of bureaucratic procedures and related institutional incentives, may give insights into the impediments to private ownership and business activity, they are difficult to interpret and to quantify in terms entrepreneurial activity frustrated. For example, easing the barrier "lack of finance" may be neither possible nor desirable if entrepreneurship is to be economically beneficial rather than simply rent seeking behaviour. Entrepreneurship (and risk taking) is, however, influenced by general institutional factors and framework conditions although they may not be noted explicitly by individuals in interviews.

Risk aversion

Risk aversion is a key factor in shaping public attitudes to entrepreneurial activity. One recent survey[67] indicated that around 13 per cent of the Austrian

Table 14. **Barriers to the planned longer-term development of small and medium-sized enterprises**

Per cent of respondents citing the item as a barrier

Country	Succession at director level	Export difficulties	Cost of financing	Insufficient demand	Lack of financing	Insufficient own funds	Difficulties raising loans	Social and fiscal charges	European legislation	R&D costs	Difficulties accessing new markets	Other
Austria	**14**	**1**	**25**	**30**	**26**	**21**	**6**	**39**	**9**	**8**	**29**	**5**
Belgium	13	4	20	29	18	9	7	38	9	6	20	5
Denmark	21	3	10	31	12	8	6	27	11	12	11	10
Finland	13	2	18	39	12	8	7	18	8	8	32	10
France	15	10	15	33	23	20	4	57	12	6	28	3
Germany	12	2	27	38	23	17	8	32	17	8	30	5
Greece	12	2	49	34	30	20	20	41	3	11	30	4
Ireland	21	6	10	24	16	9	6	24	11	6	25	6
Italy	13	6	36	36	22	9	10	46	7	7	31	5
Luxembourg	18	6	17	34	10	5	1	18	30	2	30	1
Netherlands	17	1	9	26	9	3	3	14	11	8	14	8
Portugal	12	1	29	43	10	0	9	20	9	9	23	17
Spain	14	1	32	39	16	7	9	22	5	5	30	7
Sweden	11	1	14	34	11	6	4	24	5	6	23	11
United Kingdom	29	3	19	30	16	6	10	15	16	6	18	11
EU average	15	4	25	35	20	12	8	33	10	8	28	6
Malta	12	15	23	52	6	3	6	13	6	5	29	11
Norway	15	4	18	26	22	19	4	10	3	8	17	15
Switzerland	7	9	20	37	26	15	13	30	9	4	26	10
Turkey	21	15	42	30	53	21	31	26	5	7	39	4
Overall average	**15**	4	25	35	21	12	9	33	10	8	28	6

Source: Survey of European small and medium-sized enterprises, Exco and Grant International, 1997.

population had at some stage thought about becoming self-employed and about 6 per cent had planned to become self-employed. These responses were broadly similar to those found in a comparable study for France. For those who had not considered the option of becoming self-employed, risk figures as the key factor (32 per cent) followed by finance (20 per cent) and excessive responsibility (11 per cent). Just over 40 per cent of youths (up to 25 years old) who had decided against becoming self-employed cited risk as the key factor. More importantly, however, only 5 per cent of those who planned to become self-employed actually became so (in comparison with 14 per cent in France), risk being cited as a major factor.

One reason for the apparently high risk aversion among Austrians could be the social security system, which raises the opportunity cost of making the transition to self employment. Indeed, careful policy design may be needed to find the difficult balance between risk taking and innovative activity and a highly developed system of welfare which socialises many risks. The expansion of the state itself may also have been a factor: risk aversion is high among graduates, of whom until the early 1990s over 80 per cent were absorbed by the civil service. With new job openings in the civil service declining sharply, these attitudes may be subject to gradual revision.

Recent policy measures have sought to reduce the financial consequences of risk. In order to reduce the disincentives inherent in the social security system, the government has recently extended coverage so that individuals with a right to unemployment benefits will preserve their entitlement during a period of self-employment in case the enterprise fails. A programme to help the unemployed start an enterprise was also established in 1998 after a pilot phase beginning in 1995. The unemployed can obtain financial support for training and business counselling. During the start-up phase participants receive a living allowance, so as to avoid drawing funds out of the business, and to reduce the income risk in case of a failure, the eligibility period for obtaining unemployment benefits has been extended. While 1 800 enterprises had been founded with the support of the programme by autumn 1998, no full evaluation of the programme's effectiveness is available.[68] Several other OECD countries have set up programmes to support the transition from unemployment into self employment. Evaluation studies suggests that such programmes only work for a small subset of the unemployed, and that success is largely associated with relatively high educational levels and short current unemployment spells.[69] There is also a moral hazard issue arising from the fact that participation in the programme generates new replacement income and extends the eligibility period for unemployment benefits. A recent investigation of the support programme in Germany, which appears to have similar design features to the Austrian scheme, indicates that enterprises established under such a scheme have employment creation records similar to other new start-ups, but the firm survival rate is lower.[70] Hence, evaluations of the Austrian programme will be important to judge its cost effectiveness.

Bankruptcy procedures also affect the propensity to accept entrepreneurial risk, a balance being required between the interests of creditors and the need for an efficient means of exit for unsuccessful firms. In Austria, as in Europe more generally, not only is there a stigma associated with business failure but discharge rules mean that failed entrepreneurs can be pursued for at least seven years (Table 15) which is neither conducive to risk-taking activity nor to re-entry into business life. As noted in the 1998 *Survey*, reorganisation arrangements with creditors prior to the onset of bankruptcy procedures have been introduced recently and these could support entrepreneurship through introducing greater flexibility.[71] However, they have been little used up to the present and the absence of any protection from creditors reduces their potential effectiveness. A special system of debt reorganisation has been developed in the tourist sector and this might have improved the entrepreneurial climate in the branch.

Table 15. **An international comparison of bankruptcy procedures**

Country	Filing	Discharge clause
Austria	Entrepreneurs can voluntarily file for bankruptcy.	Different kinds of discharge but in general only after seven years
Australia	Entrepreneurs can voluntarily file for bankruptcy. For limited companies a number of procedures for liquidation and voluntary administration are in place.	Discharged after three years. For negligible amounts discharge can be granted after three months. Managers are not liable unless involved in improper dealing.
Germany		Currently, no discharge. Company managers incur civil liability and may also be liable for criminal penalties. Reforms to be enacted will discharge liability companies after seven years.
Sweden	Entrepreneurs can voluntarily file for bankruptcy. However, high-priority debt must be settled, and some additional costs are involved.	No discharge. Managers and owners of limited companies can be made personally liability for tax debts.
United Kingdom		Discharged after two years if the debt is lower than £20 000; three years if the debt is greater.
United States	Entrepreneurs can voluntarily file for bankruptcy. Many bankruptcies are settled outside the courtroom.	Discharge effective immediately.

Source: Submissions from national authorities.

Contestability of markets and the level of regulation

In drawing conclusions from five case studies, the OECD's report *Fostering Entrepreneurship* stressed the importance of reducing barriers to competition and of lowering the burdens of the regulatory environment if entrepreneurship is to be fostered. These lessons are particularly relevant to the Austrian situation.

Barriers to entry have been particularly important in basic *telecommunications, electricity generation, trades occupations* and the *liberal professions*. Closed or restricted markets resulted in high prices and reduced opportunities for entrepreneurs in these and in downstream activities.[72] However, the dominant trend has been toward improvement:

- As noted in Chapter III, much has been achieved in liberalising the telecommunications sector. Deregulation and lower prices can be expected to open a wide range of opportunities for business expansion in the future both in the telecommunications sector itself and in sectors with high telecoms inputs.
- In a similar way, the opening of the electricity market should allow room for entrepreneurial activity by large firms, unless that is existing firms are able to protect their positions through regulatory means, while lower prices will increase the potential for energy intensive firms to widen their activities.
- The Trades Law was somewhat liberalised in 1997. While little time has since elapsed, there is some controversy and disappointment that a wave of new enterprise has not, as expected, materialised.[73] Indeed, although 80 trades were declared free, the remaining 84 encompass the majority of businesses. Moreover, only 21 part deregulated trades were founded and these did not include repair activities where a substantial expansion could have been expected.

On the other hand, little progress has been made in opening the public sector to competition from alternative providers in the business sector. The public sector produces a wide range of services which are not subject to tender even though prices may be substantially above those which private suppliers could offer. According to one estimate, 130 000 public sector employees are involved in what are essentially marketable activities,[74] equivalent to a turnover of about Sch 100 billion. Moreover, the pace of privatisation has slowed in the last few years although there have been several major transactions including the privatisation of a major bank (Creditanstalt), the partial sale of the tobacco company, and a placement of 25 per cent of shares in Telekom.[75]

Austria is marked by a high regulatory density, which is cited by existing firms and potential entrepreneurs alike as expensive and inefficient.[76] The legal and administrative requirements to form a limited liability company involve more time and require a larger number of procedures than in many other countries and the minimum capital required is the highest in the OECD (Figure 19). This latter requirement could discriminate against entrepreneurship since it effectively raises the threshold at which entrepreneurs can limit risk through the institution of the limited liability company.[77] Particularly important, however, have been the long and complex procedures for receiving approvals for a factory or business premises, with many different authorities and overlapping competencies. Social and labour market regulations – including opening hours for business – are also cited as an obstacle to entrepreneurial activity.

Approval procedures for establishing new business premises, changing the ownership of existing facilities or modifying existing plants (*Betriebsanlagengenehmigungsverfahren*) have repeatedly been criticised as being complicated and lengthy. A study based on a survey conducted in 1997, involving public sector authorities of fourteen European countries, concludes that average approval times in Austria[78] corresponded broadly to the European average. However, the investigation also indicated that the number of approvals per year is much higher in Austria than in other countries.[79] For example, whereas in Germany there are around 6 000 approvals per year, in Austria the volume is closer to 13 000.[80] This is attributable to the fact that in Austria even smaller installations are subject to approval requirements. In addition, authorisation often involves contacting a multitude of different public sector authorities. The investigation did not cover approvals based on environmental laws which can be particularly time consuming so that administrative requirements are greater than indicated by the study.

As noted in the last *Survey*, some progress has already been made in streamlining the procedures for approving business premises. Continuing the reform process in this field, the government has now proposed legislation (*Betriebsanlagengesetz*) to establish a "one-stop-shop" principle, although agreement is still required, and regulatory reform is to be taken up in the framework of the NAP (Box 7): one single governmental authority would be responsible for dealing with approval requests, distributing them to the public authorities charged with examining the relevant aspects of the application, authorising the project, and monitoring the compliance of the entrepreneur. Applications should be decided within three or six months, depending on the environmental significance of the request. For installations which improve emissions or leave them unchanged, decisions would need to be made within two months. According to estimates by the Ministry of Economics, this could cut significantly the number of approval procedures, mainly by suppressing parallel and overlapping processes.

Although there have been significant improvements in the regulatory environment in recent years – including an easing of shop-opening hours – there has been an important set back in the area of retailing. As noted in the 1998 *Survey*, additional restrictions have been imposed by regulations under the new

Figure 19. **Legal and administrative requirements
to form companies**[1]

A. Total number of procedures for corporate registration and maximum delay in weeks[1]

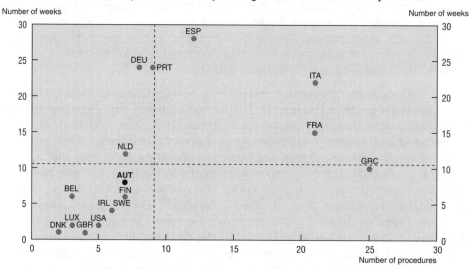

B. Minimum capital requirement for private limited companies (thousand ECU)[2]

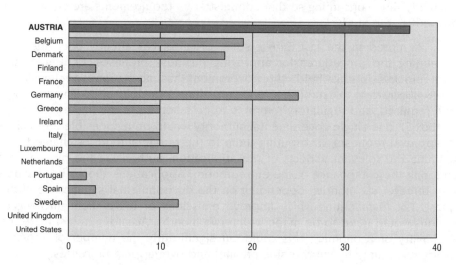

1.   In 1996.
2.   Data have been harmonised by the OECD.
3.   For Japan the minimum capital required for a stock corporation *(Kabushiki Kaisha)* amounts to 70 000 ECU.
Source: Project EIMS 96/142 Logotech S.A.; OECD.

Box 7.   **The objectives of the National Action Programme
to promote entrepreneurship**

In the National Action Plan for Employment (see Box 4 for details) the government has proposed three fields for policy action relevant to the theme entrepreneurship, indicated areas for policy initiatives and specified performance criteria.

Developing entrepreneurship (indicators: new business start-ups, time for approvals)

- *Reducing overheads and administrative costs:* easier trade regulations and approvals
- *Eliminating obstacles to self employment:* includes easier possibilities for inheriting firms, new forms of finance, advisory services
- *Creation of new jobs (particularly in the service sector):* social, nursing care and medical services to be expanded with greater use of financial transfers to create employment, easier access to social occupations and greater investment in the area. Examine ways of opening access to occupations, creation of jobs in new technologies through telecommunications deregulation, business start-up centres and support development of consultancy firms;
- *Reducing taxes and charges on labour:* tax reform.

Encouraging adaptability in business and by employees

- *Agreement by social partners on modernising work organisation:* social partners should achieve greater flexibility; overtime should be reduced and part-time work made more attractive
- *Reform of employment contracts:* support part-time work, grant equal status to manual and white collar workers
- *Investment in human resources:* investment incentives to be more oriented to employment; guarantees also to cover investment in human capital; government support for investment to be linked to willingness to train.

Promoting technology (indicator: raising level of R&D from 1.5 per cent of GDP to EU average)

- *Technology diffusion:* creation of skill centres, promote exploitation of patents, extending capital base of small and medium-sized firms by special loans; more cluster funding.

---

trades law (*Gewerbeordung*) on the establishment of large shopping centres outside of town if they endanger the operation of local shops. Approval for the establishment of new centres within ten car-minutes from a town requires *inter alia* that turnover should not exceed 5 per cent of the turnover of existing companies in the area. Approval also requires the creation of new working places. The restrictions were intended to cover local retail distribution (*Nahversorgung*), such as foodstuffs, but they have been extended to cover durable products such as furniture. Several retail chains have appealed to the Constitutional Court to declare several of the restrictions unconstitutional. The protection which such zoning restrictions give to in-town shopping is likely to be quite costly in terms of restraints on competition and on innovation thereby leading to a loss of consumer welfare.

The financial system

Entrepreneurial activity in Austria has been strongly affected by financing arrangements, but the interplay of factors which underlies this has been far from clear. When respondents state that the lack of finance is a barrier, this often refers to subsidised credit. As noted above, the fastest-growing firms do not cite lack of finance as a key barrier. Small-to-medium-sized enterprises have traditionally relied on bank finance – as have larger firms – and they have often shown a desire to avoid loss of control (and greater disclosure obligations) which greater reliance on equity or on other forms of external financing would bring. The resultant reliance on bank finance, and the close relationship with banks which this entailed, has made for rather stable business finances[81] – as well as stability in enterprise structure – but it may have been at the cost of entrepreneurial and innovative activity. As in many other countries, start-ups and innovative projects by existing firms have often been assessed more on the basis of the collateral available than on the basis of the project's merits. More importantly, though, the over-emphasis on bank mediation and self-financing (also a product of the tax system, see below) has led to the under-development of the Austrian financial markets and this might have held back entrepreneurship. There have been recent advances in this sphere, and those related to the stock exchange, including the new small company listing, are discussed in Chapter III. A great deal of attention has also been devoted to the development of the venture capital market and informal investors or business angels, both of which have been associated in other countries with developments in the high-technology area.

Venture capital

The organisational features of the formal venture capital market have been developing rapidly. There are now 20 venture capital funds based in Austria, of which eleven are domestically-owned, mainly by banks. By the end of 1996, the funds had resources of around Sch 20 billion, although only about Sch 8 billion were actually invested. In addition, there are twelve investment companies (Kapitalbeteiligungsgesellschaften), set up by the Länder, with resources of Sch 3.7 billion at the end of 1997. Of this about Sch 2.3 had already been invested. Foreign-based funds are also financing projects in Austria, but there are only around four such investments, a remarkably low figure in comparison with other European countries (70 projects in Portugal alone) and on a par with Iceland.[82] One important barrier to the development of venture capital has been the lack of an exit mechanism *via* an initial public offering on the stock exchange. However, this is slowly improving with the development on a new small company board on the Vienna exchange and with the decision to link with Frankfurt (see Chapter III). Some market participants believe that the barrier to the development of the venture capital market is more the lack of projects than the availability of finance.

Public support programmes have been remodelled in recent years to encourage venture capital funds but the situation with respect to tax is more complex. Public institutions provide a number of guarantees for medium-sized enterprises, often associated with high-technology (Box 8). A guarantee institution

---

Box 8.   Measures to support financing of start-ups
and business expansion

In addition to a wide range of often free advisory and counselling services provided by the Economics Chamber, state government organisations, and federal government organisations, there is an extremely wide range of financial programmes to cover business start-ups and the transition to the expansion phase and beyond. The programmes include:*

- Premia for savings prior to founding an enterprise or taking over an existing one; an interest rate subsidy related to the equity which must be provided when taking out a loan for a start-up.
- Loan guarantees, interest-rate-caps and investment subsidies for start-ups up to a financing volume of Sch 2 million.
- Guarantees for loss of equity investment in the case of bankruptcy for up to ten years and to a maximum of Sch 10 million per firm; guarantees for investment companies and venture capital funds to take stakes in SMEs also in the technology area (with a total value of the programme of Sch 2 billion).
- Provision of seed financing for start-ups in the area of new technology in the form of grants for consultancy and equity like loans.
- Credits for research oriented SMEs up to five years with interest paid at the end of the period and with the condition that the firm seek either a listing or other investors.
- Special loans for existing medium-sized firms to undertake research programmes to support new products or processes; interest rate of 1.5 per cent and a bonus if employment rises by more than 10 per cent and new equity in the amount of the loan must be introduced at the end of the period; similar programmes for innovative investment projects.
- Special equity participation by organisations run by the federal states including share buy back arrangements and capital guarantees.

---

* For a full description of many of the programmes see E. Kühnelt and R. Lichtmannegger, *Eigenkapitalwirksame Finanzierung*, Wirtschaftskammer, Wien, August, 1997.

(FGG) issues capital guarantees of up to 50 per cent for venture funds. A state investment bank (BÜRGES) issues project-related guarantees for private individuals for up to 100 per cent of the capital invested in the event of a bankruptcy up to Sch 260 000, and guarantees for up to 50 per cent in the event of bankruptcy up to Sch 10 million. With respect to tax incentives, there are no special breaks favouring the development of venture capital as such. However, the tax reform of 1993 introduced incentives to encourage the development of funds specialising in providing finance to and taking minority holdings in medium-sized companies operating mainly in Austria (*Mittelstandsfinanzierungsgesellschaften*). For five years after their establishment such funds are exempt from corporation tax, and after that capital gains from realising investments are also tax free. Investors are also exempt from paying capital earnings taxes up to a limit of Sch 200 000. The tax rules for the more usual investment funds are neutral in the sense that an investment *via* such funds is treated the same way as a direct purchase of a bond or a share. There is an advantage, however, in that capital gains can be realised tax free without having to observe the minimum holding period of one year. There is a bias against venture capital insofar, as to protect investors, a general investment fund is not allowed to purchase "risky capital" which effectively precludes non-listed companies. In addition, pension funds remain underdeveloped but investments would, in any case, remain restricted by current regulations. For a company buying and selling venture capital investments, the capital gains would be taxable. In sum, the tax system is fairly neutral with direct government programmes serving as a substitute for tax breaks which are more usual in a number of other countries.

Informal investors

"Business angels" – who not only provide equity finance but also take a direct role in advising the firm, often on the basis of their own extensive experience – have developed spontaneously in many countries. In Austria the government has taken the initiative, and has been operating a business-angel exchange through the Innovation Agency since the end of 1996. In that time, 100 contacts between investors and enterprises have been facilitated and four projects have been completed, up to the stage of registering the new company. Others are soon to reach this final stage. Thirty-seven investors are registered of which 60 per cent are private persons, most of whom also wish to actively participate in the company. Some intermediaries such as accountants and lawyers are also participating, so that there are in effect around 100 investors including venture funds and other companies which will also act as "angels". Of the companies seeking finance, 40 per cent are in the microelectronics area and 15 per cent in environmental technologies and over 90 per cent of them welcomed active investor participation – at least at this early stage.

Equity finance and start-up funding

In addition to the schemes mentioned above, there are a wide range of financial programmes provided by state-backed institutions designed to encourage equity finance of companies, in either the start-up or expansion phase. A number of measures are confined to high-technology companies. In mid 1997, the total value of guarantees and funds available amounted to some Sch 10 billion and this has increased in the meantime with new programmes. An overview of some programmes is given in Box 8.[83]

Taxation and social charges

The high level of social charges is sometimes cited as an impediment to entrepreneurship and business expansion although how high labour costs *per se* might act as a general barrier to innovation is unclear. However, in contrast to many other countries, the self-employed are members of the social security system and are therefore liable for private contributions to the scheme. This has often been a severe drain on an enterprise's liquidity during the grounding phase, and could have reduced start-up activity. As from the beginning of 1999, social security contributions by the self-employed during the first year of operations will be reduced, thereby relieving part of this financial burden.

The corporate and personal tax system in place up to the early 1990s did not aid the development of an entrepreneurial culture. Until 1988 the highest personal marginal tax rate was 62 per cent and the corporate tax was progressive, with a top rate of 55 per cent. Dividends received by companies were also subject to the tax, while there was a wealth tax and a tax of 2 per cent on new equity. As indicated in the 1997 Survey, the corporate tax wedge was also significant, with retained earnings subject to a high effective tax while debt financing was subject to a negative tax. Debt finance was thus the tax-preferred option, reinforcing the predominance of bank intermediation. As documented in the previous Survey, the situation has improved dramatically with the major tax reforms of 1988 and 1993, so that the corporate tax wedge has been much reduced and made more uniform with respect to sources of finance. The wealth tax has been abolished. Such changes may take some time to affect perceptions among the population that taxation is a barrier to entrepreneurship; these are often based on misconceptions and a general reticence in dealing with the authorities since taxation has a smaller effect on behaviour the further entrepreneurs move into the preparation stage of a project. However, the top rate of personal tax (50 per cent) may still constitute a disincentive to entrepreneurial activity, and the 1998 *Economic Survey* concluded that there were still incentives for companies to maintain a low level of equity capital (thin capitalisation) which might hinder the development of new dynamic companies.

A framework condition which could affect the entrepreneurial climate negatively is the tax treatment of ownership transfer in existing enterprises. In contrast to the situation in a number of other countries, there are no special provisions in the inheritance and gift tax regulations linked to the continuation of an enterprise, although the Tax Reform Commission has recommended reforms which have now been taken up in the government's proposed tax reform (Chapter II). This is potentially a major problem, since some 30 000 to 50 000 enterprises will need to change hands for demographic reasons in the coming three to five years. The argument is not, however, clear-cut since it is not evident that heirs and successors are entrepreneurial – as opposed to self-employed. Indeed, it might be preferable to force enterprises onto the market for ownership. To be effective, financial markets would need to be efficient, particularly in this segment. Clearly this is not the case so that changing the tax laws in favour of transfers would constitute a second best policy.

Development and diffusion of technology

The moderate level of technological innovation in Austria, noted in the first section, is in part a function of the more general barriers to entrepreneurship discussed above such as regulation, market opportunities, financial arrangements and taxation.[84] However, it is also a function of more specific institutional arrangements and policy settings which together have combined to produce a weak national innovation system. In response, there have been a number of policy initiatives to foster the diffusion of technology (Box 9) although the political debate has often focused more on support to R&D. It is difficult at this stage to assess the cost effectiveness of the programmes.

A key weakness of the national innovation system is the universities. The Austrian education system is oriented towards middle-level qualifications, so that the number in tertiary education is below the OECD average. Universities absorb the bulk of public R&D funding, which is high by international standards but for which investment returns are low. Universities have little contact with the business sector – the proportion of research contracted out by enterprises is the lowest in the OECD and the research interests of the universities do not correspond to the industrial structure – and the funding from abroad is lower than in other small open economies and beneath the EU average.[85] One reason for this low productivity is that the university funding system gives little incentive for universities to acquire extra income, since it would only be offset against their government grants. Another and probably more important factor is the tenure of professors and an emphasis on academic activities in defining success. In addition, the university system has also had great difficulty reallocating resources to new or expanding faculties. This may have contributed to the low numbers of graduating engineers and scientists which in turn means that there are only

---

Box 9.   Policies to foster technology diffusion

In addition to providing financial support for technology oriented business start ups and for innovative business expansion, (Box 8), the Austrian government has implemented a number of policies to support technological innovation and diffusion and intends to widen these efforts in the context of the NAP. The programmes include:

Technology diffusion: the MINT programme supports around 200 SMEs defined as those with between 50 and 250 employees and aims to strengthen innovation and promote the introduction of new technologies. The programme involves supporting and developing consulting activities to improve the capability of management to identify problems and to manage the introduction of new technologies. The scheme is based on the Norwegian BUNT programme.*

Technology incubators: incubators are the responsibility of technology and innovation centres (of which there are 28) which are usually run by the states. The centre in Vienna has helped create 37 firms since 1988 of which 35 have survived employing around 200 persons.

Integrating science and industry:

The government's Industrial Research Promotion Fund (FFF) has been commissioned by the Ministry of Science to implement joint programmes between the new polytechnics and enterprises (mainly SMEs) since 1997. Depending on the project size, 20 to 30 per cent of private funding is mandatory and federal funding can cover up to 50 per cent of the overall costs of the project and the remainder from regional authorities. Projects are approved by a panel of international experts. The programme has disbursed some Sch 40 million to date. A new round of proposals will be called this year with a value of Sch 50 million.

A programme to establish competence centres aims to better integrate the work of universities and industry through new collaborative institutions of which ten to twenty are to be established. Public funds will finance up to 60 per cent of the budget of the centres and a minimum of 40 per cent has to be financed by at least five strategic partners. Five centres were approved in 1998 after an international selection process. Another five will most likely be approved for funding in 1999.

In addition, there is a scheme to subsidise the employment of post doctoral research workers in industry and a new institution is being established to promote the commercialisation of university research.

---

* See *Diffusing technology to industry: government policies and programmes*, OECD, Paris, 1997, for more details.

---

34 researchers per 10 000 of the labour force (Table 16). The small proportion of technical graduates may account in part for the low level of interest by graduates in entrepreneurial activity noted above.

Table 16.   **Researchers by sector of employment**[1]

	Business enterprise	Government	Higher Education	Total researchers per 10 000 labour force
	Percentage			
United States[2]	79	6	13	74
Japan	65	5	28	92
Germany[3]	56	16	28	59
France	44	18	35	60
Italy[3]	36	18	46	32
United Kingdom	56	9	33	50
Canada[3]	54	7	38	54
Australia	25	15	58	66
Austria[2]	**55**	**7**	**38**	**34**
Belgium[3]	51	4	43	53
Czech Republic	37	35	27	25
Denmark	41	23	35	58
Finland[3]	40	21	38	67
Greece[2]	16	24	59	20
Hungary	25	38	37	26
Iceland	35	39	25	61
Ireland[3]	40	3	54	58
Mexico[3]	10	31	58	6
Netherlands	40	23	36	46
New Zealand[3]	26	25	50	35
Norway[3]	50	19	31	73
Poland	20	21	59	31
Portugal[3]	8	24	46	24
Spain	21	18	60	32
Sweden[3]	57	8	35	78
Switzerland	58	3	40	55
Turkey	14	13	73	8

1.   Data refer to 1996 unless otherwise noted.
2.   Data refer to 1993.
3.   Data refer to 1995.
Source: OECD (1998), Main Science and Technology Indicators.

Assessment and agenda for policy action

When viewed against the recent past, entrepreneurial activity has become more pronounced in recent years in Austria. The private business sector has become the principal engine of growth, the rate of new start-ups has picked up and a number of fast-growing firms have emerged. A rudimentary risk capital market has begun to develop and innovative activity, as reflected in technological diffusion and external R&D contacts, has strengthened. At the same time, public attitudes to enterprises have been changing, with job creation being less linked in popular perception to public sector job creation and more to personal initiative. This shift in attitudes could prove self reinforcing, since one study[86] has found that just over half of potential entrepreneurs (business founders) were influenced by a role model and that there was a positive relationship between having such an example and actually establishing an enterprise. However, measured against the challenges facing the economy – and the developments in other countries – entrepreneurship would appear to need strengthening, both to underpin a wider strategy to promote additional employment and to create a base for stronger business-sector productivity growth in the coming decades when the population will be ageing.

Since entrepreneurship, very broadly defined, is a complex cultural/social phenomena whose determinants are rooted in traditions and institutions, policy responses need to remain country specific and lessons from international practice will not always apply.[87] There is, however, compelling evidence that framework conditions are important for fostering entrepreneurship, so that the OECD has been led to define broad policy guidelines in this area. In general, there is a presumption that governments should concern themselves to establish an overall institutional framework which would provide maximum scope for entrepreneurship to flourish. Priorities here include promoting competition in all sectors, ensuring efficient financial markets and reducing the administrative and regulatory burdens of government including promoting an efficient tax system. Only thereafter is there a role for specific policies to promote entrepreneurship. These need to be based on a broad definition of entrepreneurship. There is no compelling evidence that policies which seek directly to stimulate entrepreneurship (and hence innovation) by socialising risks (through instruments such as public guarantees and soft loans) can, or will, be successful. Various forms of rent-seeking activity are usually stimulated but not entrepreneurship in the proper sense. Although significant policy advances have been achieved, this chapter has identified the need for action in several areas: market opening and regulatory reform in product and service markets, the financial system, the reduction of unnecessary risk and the university system. Flexible labour markets are also important, as indicated by the policy requirements discussed in Chapter III.

With respect to market opening and deregulation, there has been significant progress in several areas, especially telecommunications, and the National Action Programme pushes forward the process in a more general way. There are a number of priorities for further action which are summarised in Box 5:

   – Although the liberalisation of the trades law (*Gewerbeordnung*) in 1997 was an advance, further liberalisation remains necessary and the number of part-regulated trades could be radically increased – a proposal rejected by the social partners in 1997. The concern to avoid a dilution of the training system is legitimate but the value of qualifications to those receiving them – and the returns to those giving the training – can and should be protected in other ways than through reducing entry.

– The "one-stop shop" approach to approvals of business places needs to be implemented but to be fully effective there would also need to be a substantial decline in regulatory barriers and procedures more generally.

– The restrictive conditions applying to opening large shopping centres threaten to stop innovation in that sector. Shop opening hours – and business hours more generally – remain restrictive and could be further liberalised.

– The self provision of goods and services by the public sector needs to be curtailed or at least subjected to genuine competition from private suppliers.

– Consideration needs to be given to liberalising access to the liberal professions.

Austrian financial markets are continuing to develop, with the stock exchange becoming more closely linked to the Frankfurt exchange and a system of venture capital funds coming into place. At the same time, a large number of public programmes have been established to provide funds to small and medium-sized firms, and to high-technology firms in particular. A number of dangers are in principle associated with public programmes. It is extremely important that public guarantees and funds do not displace private funding and misdirect entrepreneurial effort. In this respect some programmes are better than others, especially those which specify financial penalties if new equity is not introduced at the end of the loan. While it is important to help establish well-functioning capital markets, public support programmes should not seek to directly create entrepreneurs. In any case, it is not clear that lack of finance is the crucial factor in entrepreneurial development: a lack of ideas and of profitable projects could be of equal importance. Government measures should thus remain focused on broader framework conditions such as market opening and regulatory reform.

Following several reforms during the last decade, the tax system represents less of a barrier to entrepreneurial activity than was previously the case. However, several areas are still in need of reform and need to be considered in the coming round of tax reform. At 50 per cent, the top personal tax rate remains high, while equity capital is still not treated on par with loans for the purposes of taxation. Moreover, the tax legislation covering the take-over of existing firms – either by purchase or inheritance – might need to be reviewed.

The university system represents a weak link in several respects: given the amount of R&D funding allocated to it, productivity appears low and universities are poorly connected to other aspects of the national innovation system. The system produces too few graduates in sciences and engineering and the entrepreneurial orientation of graduates appears to be weaker than in many other countries. Some of these features are clearly cultural, but could be expected to change over time if the framework conditions alter. To this end, added momentum needs to be given to implementing university reform in order to make them more competitive and to allow rewards for success, through for example permitting funds gained from patents and spin-offs to be retained. The government intends to promote skill centres and create an agency to assist in commercialising patents but for these to be fully effective, and to avoid institutional capture by existing universities, more fundamental reforms will be necessary.

Although legislation cannot alter the public stigma attached to bankruptcy policy, it could, nevertheless, reduce some of the excessive risks associated with the present system. In particular, consideration could be given to a general discharge and for the possibility of allowing debtors to re-enter commercial life with the minimum of delay compatible with ethical business practice.

The need to foster entrepreneurship has been recognised by both the government and the social partners and forms an important plank of the National Action Programme which has been submitted to the Council of Ministers of the EU. Many of the proposals in the programme go in the direction of the recommendations presented here. However, some of the commitments in the Programme lack specific detail, so that it is not clear how they will be actually implemented. Any tendency to avoid more difficult institutional reform and changes in framework conditions in favour of direct devices (*e.g.* make work programmes) to raise employment – the proximate objective of the Programme – will need to be held in check. Entrepreneurship is the key to a dynamic economy so that finding an appropriate balance between risk-taking, innovative behaviour and the desire for a consensus-based, stable, social economy will remain the greatest challenge in the years ahead.

Notes

1. The decline in public consumption in 1997 by 3.9 per cent in real terms was in great measure due to a new system of reimbursing hospitals which led to a reclassification from public consumption to transfers. It was also due to the reclassification of a number of federal, state and local entities from the public to the corporate sector. See Chapter II for details.

2. M. Wüger, "Kräftiges Konsumwachstum bei Steigender Sparquote", WIFO *Monatsberichte*, 12/1998.

3. M. Scheiblecker, "Wachsende Inlandsnachfrage, Aber Abschwächung Im Export", WIFO *Monatsberichte*, 2/1999.

4. The collective agreement in the metal industry provided for a 2.9 per cent wage rise and for ½ per cent as a lump-sum payment.

5. *Economic Outlook*, 64, December, 1998, OECD, Paris.

6. Italy, which had higher rates than the other European countries, lowered its key rate to 3.5 per cent.

7. The rates for the other policy instruments (*Gomex*, discount and *Lombard*) remained unchanged.

8. The currency reserves transferred by the OeNB to the ECB amounted to Sch 16.4 billion.

9. A major change to the financial system is that commercial banks can no longer endorse bills of exchange (*Wechsel*) with the central bank for a discount. The discount facility, which was a feature of the Austrian (and German) refinancing system, was used extensively by credit institutions for refinance and the volume totalled about 80 per cent of the volume of repurchase operations (1997). However, the consequences for liquidity management by banks is limited since bills of exchange are still recognised as collateral for central bank credits.

10. Based on past reserve holdings and present interest rates, the remuneration is estimated to amount to about Sch 1.7 billion per year.

11. An alternative scenario where all downside risks are assumed to occur at the same time was presented in *Economic Outlook* 64, December 1998.

12. Under EU legislation the participants in the EU Monetary Union are obliged to present an annual Stability Programme for a four-year horizon, outlining the projected fiscal stance and targets as well as the government's assessment of economic growth prospects.

13. In March 1999 the official projection was revised downwards to 2¼ per cent.

14. The direct budgetary risks from the financial crisis in Russia should be limited. Contingent liabilities of the Austrian government and assets at risk total about

Sch 36.5 billion, almost all of which are obligations which Russia took over from the former Soviet Union. Until 2002 debt servicing consists solely of interest payments, and debt redemption will be spread out between 2002 and 2020.

15. The government projects real growth to slow gradually from 3.3 per cent in 1998 to 2.1 per cent in 2001, recovering slightly to 2.2 per cent in 2002.

16. In these simulations disturbances of the economic environment comprise real supply shocks, real private demand shocks and nominal shocks. For details see Dalsgaard, Thomas and Alain de Serres: "Estimating Prudent Budgetary Margins for 11 EU Countries: A simulated SVAR model approach", OECD *Economics Department Working Papers* (1999 forthcoming).

17. For a discussion of these problems, see OECD *Economic Survey of Austria*, 1994.

18. After a transition period for phasing in the new measures the legislated amendments are estimated to generate savings relative to baseline amounting to $1^1/_2$ per cent of GDP; estimates by the government suggest that, with unchanged policies, pension outlays would have risen by $4^1/_2$ per cent of GDP by 2030. As a result, pension outlays will still rise by 3 per cent of GDP.

19. Annual pension adjustments broadly follow the development of wages net of social security contributions. As part of the fiscal consolidation package, in 1997 pension adjustment was suspended.

20. See OECD, *Education at a Glance*, Paris 1998.

21. The council will consist of the Federal Chancellor, the Vice-Chancellor, the Federal Minister of Finance, members of the Länder governments and one representative each of the two local authority associations.

22. See OECD, *Economic Survey of Austria*, 1994.

23. Empirical research for the United States indicates that the degree of fiscal consolidation depends on the stringency of budget caps. States with balanced budget requirements which do not allow carrying-over fiscal deficits from one year to the next have higher surpluses. See H. Bohn and R. Inman, "Balanced budget rules and public deficits: evidence from the US states", *Carnegie-Rochester Conference series on Public Policy* 45, 1966.

24. See OECD *Economic Survey of Austria*, 1997.

25. According to the *Lebensunterhaltskonzept* of the Central Statistical Office. The figure is 15 per cent according to the Labour Force concept.

26. See Micro-census of March 1998 conducted by the Central Statistical Office.

27. 63 per cent of the firms, representing 21 per cent of the sector's work force did not respond, and 31 per cent of the firms, representing 57 per cent of the workers reported no deviation from the collectively agreed wage rate.

28. The complexity of working time regulations was highlighted by a recent debate as to whether, in contrast to past practice, sun-tanning parlours should be forced to close on Saturdays and Sundays. The parlours, which are largely frequented at the week-end, are considered as "leisure institutions" and therefore allowed to open during the week-end. The legal base for their assignment to this category was challenged, unsuccessfully.

29. See the 1998 OECD *Economic Survey of Austria* for details.

30. See OECD *Economic Survey of Austria*, 1998.

31. See OECD *Economic Survey of Austria*, 1998.

32. Working hours for apprentices were liberalised in 1997, and the qualifications required for training apprentices were eased. See OECD *Economic Survey of Austria*, 1998.

33. See OECD *Economic Survey of Austria*, 1998.

34. See OECD *Economic Survey of Austria*, 1997.

35. All generators claim that insufficient allowances were made by the government to recover "stranded costs" for past investments which become obsolete under the new competitive conditions. Sch 8.7 billion of the stranded costs have been notified by the government with the EU. This amount, which will mostly accrue to the federally owned *Verbundgesellschaft* (which operates Austria's high voltage network) is only a portion of the claims that have been made by both the *Verbundgesellschaft* and the utilities of the Länder and communities. With respect to stranded costs related to the utilisation of brown coal, the Minister of Economic Affairs issued a decree in February 1999 setting the volume of stranded costs at Sch 2.43 billion. This sum will be collected from eligible customers by imposing a fee of Sch 0.00574 per kWh over a period of ten years. The authorisation by the European Commission is still pending. A decree concerning stranded investment in hydropower will be issued as soon as the relevant decisions will have been taken by the European Commission.

36. For a discussion of both approaches see OECD *Economic Survey of Austria*, 1998.

37. Some anti-competitive activities such as collusion in bidding for contracts are dealt with under the criminal law when they can be classed as fraud. In a recent case concerning bid rigging in the construction industry the courts ruled that fraud had been committed and sentenced one person to seven years imprisonment. However, fraud is often difficult to prove so that criminal law is not a substitute for effective sanctions against anti-competitive behaviour.

38. The example cited may be a case in point. Independent competition offices generally prefer structural solutions rather than remedies requiring the kind of ongoing monitoring that a market share ceiling would necessitate. They also tend to prefer solutions which leave firms a strong incentive to compete based on superior efficiency. A market share ceiling tends to undermine that incentive and may have the perverse effect of restricting the share of the most efficient player. Interestingly, the European Commission decided to allow the merger but required that most outlets in food retailing in eastern Austria be sold. The result will be that the merged firm will have a market share considerably below the earlier referred to negotiated ceiling.

39. See Fay, Robert G., "Enhancing the Effectiveness of Active Labour Market Policies: Evidence from Programme Evaluations in OECD Countries", *Labour Market and Social Policy Occasional Papers* No. 18, OECD, 1996.

40. C. Gassauer-Fleissner and W. Kalny, "Deregulierungsbedarf im Zuge einer Unternehmensgründung", S.O.S. *im Regelwald*, D. Neumann-Spallart (ed.), Vienna, 1996.

41. Although Austria has a population of only around 8 million, Austrians are well represented at the highest levels of large international corporations such as *Deutsche Telekom*, *Nestle*, HK *Shipping Lines* and *Novartis*. There are also examples of individual entrepreneurs making their mark on the world scene. For example, the founder of the Magna Corporation, which by the early 1990s had become one of the world's major car parts producers with sales of more than $6 billion and 50 000 employees world-wide, emigrated in his twenties to Canada.

42. A new law was proposed by the government at the end of 1997 to more closely control political appointments to public corporations. The bill was not enacted by the parliament.

43. *Repräsentative Meinungsumfrage zum* Thema: *"Unternehmertum"*, Markforschungsinstitut Fessel-GfK, Wien, 1998.

44. Since there are no official statistics on business start-ups, three other sources are used instead. First, with membership of economic chambers compulsory in Austria the number of new registrations is often taken as a proxy. However, there are many other reasons for a new registration and one study indicates that only around 40 per cent are indeed new start-ups. Second, there is the company registry. However, many new enterprises do not adopt the company form and registered companies are often just shells for legal reasons. Third, new registrations with the social security can also be used but these track only plants and not business enterprises as such and are also sensitive to changing corporate structure. Moreover, social security data cover only units with at least one salaried employee.

45. Herta Wanzenböck, *Das österreichische Gründungsgeschehen*, Institut fur Betriebswirtschaftslehre der Klein- und Mittelbetriebe, Wien, 1998.

46. *Op. cit.*, p. 143.

47. Institut für Gewerbe- und Handwerksforschung, *Motivation von Wiener Meisterprüfungsabsolventen für eine Unternehmertätigkeit* 1997, Wien, 1998.

48. It is argued that in countries with a low level of GDP per capita, wages will be particularly low in the service sector leading to a large number of small and perhaps informal enterprises. With higher wage costs such services would be organised more formally, thereby reducing the registered number of self employed. A counter argument would run that, with higher per capita income, the demand for services would rise and with technological change these would often be provided in the form of self-employed enterprise.

49. *Op. cit.* p. 35. Over the period 1990-1994 the number of start-ups per 1 000 employed was 8.6 in manufacturing, 30 in construction, 45 in retailing and 15 in services.

50. *Regionale Aspekte von Unternehmensgründungen in Österreich*, ZEW/Seibersdorf, 1998.

51. Defined as start ups in manufacturing and in services in branches defined as high technology rather than on the basis of information about whether the enterprise is in fact a high technology company. The industry classification used is, however, quite detailed (five digit level) so that the difference between the concepts might not be great. Engeln, *op. cit.* p. 113.

52. The share of high tech firms (rather than firms in a branch) in total start ups appears to be between 1 and 6 per cent in other countries. OECD, *Meeting of the Industry Committee at Ministerial Level – Scoreboard of Indicators*, February 1998.

53. Engeln, *op. cit.* p. 110 and Chapter 6.

54. Engeln, *op. cit.* Table 6.7.

55. Table 11 needs to be interpreted with care since it reports the size distribution of enterprises. If smaller companies failed more often than larger ones the proportion of larger firms would rise but it would not indicate growth. The study, however, indicates that this was not in general true so that the table does reflect enterprise growth.

56. Not all firms are covered, the emphasis being on medium-sized companies and 15 per cent of the equity must be held by the entrepreneur.

57. *Industrie*, No. 46, November 1998, p. 6.

58. Another more detailed study has calculated that firms started in 1990 created 44 000 jobs after five years which, if start-ups in the interim period are taken into account, would yield an appreciable though perhaps smaller estimate. Wanzenböck, *op. cit.*

59. *Employment Outlook*, OECD, 1996, Table 5.1.

60. C. Lettmayer, T. Oberholzner and S. Sheikh, "Der Beitrag dynamischer Unternehmen zur Beschäftigungsentwicklung", *Wirtschaftspolitischeblätter*, 5, 1997. In six of nineteen branches the effect on net employment was quite marked.

61. The number of Austrian foreign direct investors has risen from 679 in 1990 to 897 in 1996 and the level of investments has tripled, with Hungary now the single most important destination. "Austrian outward and inward direct investment at the end of 1996", Supplement to *Focus on Austria* 3/1998, Oesterreichische Nationalbank, Vienna.

62. *Survey of European Small and Medium-Size Enterprises*, Grant Thornton.

63. It is often argued that the ratio of R&D is influenced by the size of the country since there might be important economies of scale and scope. However, even making some allowance for size, the ratio appears low.

64. G. Hutschenreiter *et al.*, *Österreichischer Technologiebericht* 1997, TIP, Vienna, 1997.

65. Lettmayr, *op. cit.*

66. Institut für Gewerbe und Handwerksforschung, *Barrieren für potentielle Unternehmensgründer*, Vienna, 1996.

67. Institut für Gewerbe und Handwerksforschung, *Barrieren für potentielle Unternehmensgründer*, Wien, 1996.

68. For a description of the experience from the pilot programme see K. Zehetner, "Unternehmensgründung mit dem Arbeitsmarktservice Österreich und der ÖSB-Unternehmensberatung Gesellschaft M.B.H" in H. Handler (editor), *Wirtschaftsstandort Österreich: Rahmenbedingungen im Umbruch*, Wien, 1998.

69. See Fay, Robert G., "Enhancing the effectiveness of active labour market policies: evidence from programme evaluations in OECD countries", OECD *Labour market and social policy occasional papers* No. 18, 1996.

70. See Pfeiffer, F., and F. Reize, "Business start-ups by the unemployed – an econometric analysis based on firm data", ZEW *Discussion Paper* No. 19-38, Mannheim 1998.

71. The reverse might in fact be happening. It is now reported that by avoiding the request for a restructuring programme with the courts, a number of entrepreneurs are now no longer protected by limited liability and are personally liable for all debts.

72. B. Felderer *et al.*, *Re-regulierung der Freien Berufe*, Institute for Advanced Studies, Wien, October 1998.

73. This might be due to the fact that the Trades Law is considered to be only one of a number of barriers by potential entrepreneurs (Figures 16).

74. Institut für Gewerbe und Handwerksforschung, *Barrieren für potentielle Unternehmensgründer*, Wien, 1996. Quoting another source they argued that the services were 30 to 200 per cent more expensive than the private sector.

75. The value of privatisations reached some $2 billion in 1997 after $1.3 billion in 1996. The Creditanstalt was sold to Bank Austria which is in turn held by a foundation

controlled by the city of Vienna. There was a political agreement at the time that
Vienna would reduce its holding in the future. See "Privatisation: Recent Trends", in
Financial Market Trends, No. 70, 1998, OECD.

76. K. Aiginger and M. Peneder, "Reform des Österreichischen Regulierungssystems" in
     H. Handler (editor), *Wirtschaftsstandort Österreich: Rahmenbedingungen im Umbruch*, Wien,
     1998.

77. The legal requirements might also account for the fact that the limited liability firm is
     only chosen by around 13 per cent of start-ups.

78. This refers to procedures under the Trades Law (*Gewerbeordnung*). It needs to be
     stressed that this aspect of the law covers all activities and is not confined to business
     trades which other aspects of the law regulate.

79. Steiner, Gerhard, "Die Dauer von Betriebsanlagengenehmigungsverfahren im
     europäischen Vergleich, Industriellenvereinigung", Vienna 1997, mimeo.

80. A. Helmel, "Österreich braucht eine Gründungsoffensive", *Wirtschaftspolitischeblätter*, 5,
     1997.

81. M. Quehenberger, "The influence of the Oesterreichische Nationalbank on the finan-
     cing conditions of Austrian enterprises", *Focus on Austria*, 3/1997.

82. A *Survey of Venture Capital and Private Equity in Europe*, European Venture Capital Associa-
     tion, 1997. Only projects involving loans greater than a threshold are reported which
     might account for the difference in the number of projects reported by the ECVA and
     those reported by national programmes.

83. For a detailed description of these programmes see E. Kühnelt and R. Lichtmanneg-
     ger, *Eigenkapitalwirksame Finanzierung*, Wirtschaftskammer, Wien, August 1997.

84. The argument is that the tax system serves to reduce overall entrepreneurship. With
     respect to R&D activities the tax wedge is negative so that investment in this activity
     is favoured relative to, for example, investment in machinery. K. Gordon and
     H. Tchilinguirian, "Marginal effective tax rates on physical, human and R&D capital",
     OECD *Economics Department Working Papers*, No. 199, 1998.

85. Hutschenreiter, *et al.*, "Österreichs Innovationssystem im Internationalen Vergleich",
     WIFO *Monatsberichte*, 7/1998.

86. Institut für Gewerbe- und Handwerksforschung, *Barrieren für potentielle Unternehmen-
     sgründer*, Wien, 1996, p. 4.

87. *Fostering entrepreneurship*, OECD, Paris, 1998.

Annex

Chronology of main economic events

1998

January

New legislation comes into force restructuring the Vienna Stock exchange into a private stock company.

February

Reform of family support agreed costing Sch 6 billion in 1999 and Sch 12 billion annually from 2000.

March

The revised investment funds law (*Investmentfondsgesetz*) comes into force extending the range of permitted financial investments.

April

Austria submits to the EU Commission the National Action Plan for Employment.

May

The federal budget for 1999 passes parliament, projecting a deficit of Sch 70.1 billion, Sch 2.8 billion more than budgeted for 1998.

In the chemical industry, a tariff agreement comes into force which increases effective wages (*Istlöhne*) by 2.2 per cent. In construction, collective wages increase by 2 per cent.

July

Austria assumes the Presidency of the Council of the European Union for the first time since its accession in 1995.

November

The Tax Reform Commission, set up by the government, presents various options for tax reform, focusing on lowering non-wage labour costs, reducing tax exemptions, and simplifying the tax system.

The wage agreement in the metal industry determines wage increases of $3\frac{1}{2}$ per cent. Subsequently, other sectors settle for increases of around $2\frac{3}{4}$ per cent.

December

The Oesterreichische Nationalbank lowers its key policy rate (tender) from 3.2 per cent to 3.0 per cent in a co-ordinated action with the central banks participating in the EMU. Subsequently, the *Gomex*-rate for short-term open market operations is lowered by 20 basis points.

1999

January

The first phase of the revised family benefit system comes into force, extending child tax credits and cash benefits.

The conversion rate of the Schilling to the euro is set at Sch 13.7603 per euro and the responsibility for setting monetary policy is shifted from the Oesterreichische Nationalbank to the European Central Bank.

The Stability Programme specifying budgetary targets to 2002 is approved by the Council of the Ministers of the EU. The Council notes, however, that the programme lacks ambition.

February

In accordance with the EU directive, a new law for the electricity sector (*Elektrizitätswirtschafts-und-organisationsgesetz*, ELWOG) came into force in February 1999, designed to partially open the sector to competition from February 1999 onwards.

STATISTICAL ANNEX AND STRUCTURAL INDICATORS

Table A. **Gross domestic product**

Sch billion

	1988	1989	1990	1991	1992	1993	1994	1995	1996	1997	1998
	At current prices										
Expenditure											
Private consumption	886.0	943.3	1 013.0	1 073.0	1 147.7	1 194.1	1 255.1	1 311.1	1 375.1	1 413.4	1 449.8
Public consumption	302.5	319.6	338.1	367.8	398.3	429.6	455.0	469.4	480.3	478.2	493.4
Gross domestic fixed capital formation	309.1	327.8	354.1	386.1	422.0	466.3	483.4	485.1	533.3	554.1	576.8
Construction[1]	199.6	216.3	237.5	266.0	285.4	299.9	329.5	342.7	356.6	369.5	383.0
Machinery and equipment[1]	154.5	169.8	184.5	200.3	198.0	185.2	203.6	211.3	216.4	226.3	245.0
Change of stocks, incl. statistical errors	14.9	11.5	17.0	22.0	8.2	2.7	-1.1	3.8	0.5	41.4	45.4
Exports of goods and services	590.8	669.6	728.3	774.7	791.6	786.5	838.8	900.9	967.7	1 064.6	1 151.5
less: Imports of goods and services	582.6	653.4	704.9	758.0	772.0	772.6	843.0	910.5	982.0	1 079.1	1 145.6
Gross domestic product at market prices	1 565.8	1 676.7	1 813.5	1 945.8	2 057.3	2 125.3	2 237.9	2 328.7	2 414.6	2 514.4	2 622.6
Origin by sector											
Agriculture, forestry and fishing	49.0	52.3	56.6	53.0	50.0	47.3	50.4	35.7	34.0	34.9	35.6
Manufacturing and mining	392.0	413.6	437.2	469.4	498.2	507.9	504.7	524.1	541.2	556.1	592.9
Construction	95.6	103.0	114.9	130.2	140.0	149.5	165.3	169.8	180.2	188.6	195.3
Trade	212.6	228.1	249.5	264.2	278.4	277.5	287.1	313.4	322.7	328.9	337.0
Other	816.6	879.8	955.2	1 029.0	1 090.6	1 143.0	1 230.4	1 285.8	1 336.5	1 405.9	1 461.8
	At 1983 prices										
Expenditure											
Private consumption	783.2	812.0	842.5	866.5	892.2	898.5	914.6	941.0	959.8	966.9	982.9
Public consumption	248.2	251.7	254.9	260.6	265.8	273.1	279.8	279.7	281.4	270.5	273.9
Gross domestic fixed capital formation	321.1	341.2	363.7	386.6	387.1	379.4	411.1	416.0	426.5	438.3	460.0
Construction[1]	176.5	185.1	197.8	209.9	216.5	220.5	235.1	237.7	242.5	245.4	252.5
Machinery and equipment[1]	144.6	156.1	165.9	176.7	170.6	158.9	176.0	178.3	183.9	192.9	207.5
Change of stocks, incl. statistical errors	14.1	3.0	7.3	8.0	-2.3	4.7	6.1	6.2	3.9	26.8	29.4
Exports of goods and services	561.6	625.3	674.5	714.4	726.3	716.9	757.0	806.0	861.5	948.4	1 025.8
less: Imports of goods and services	565.5	612.8	657.8	700.3	712.9	708.2	766.9	820.2	872.1	948.0	1 013.8
Gross domestic product at market prices	1 362.7	1 420.3	1 485.0	1 535.8	1 556.4	1 564.4	1 601.7	1 628.7	1 661.0	1 702.8	1 758.2
Origin by sector											
Agriculture, forestry and fishing	46.5	46.2	48.1	44.9	43.6	43.5	45.7	44.1	44.2	44.6	44.6
Manufacturing and mining	370.2	381.3	398.2	414.8	430.0	429.7	422.0	431.7	438.1	444.1	465.9
Construction	84.1	87.6	92.0	98.0	100.7	103.2	111.0	111.0	114.2	116.5	120.0
Trade	202.3	212.3	226.1	235.1	236.9	235.7	238.8	253.7	258.5	263.4	269.4
Other	659.6	692.9	720.7	743.0	745.2	752.3	784.2	788.2	805.9	834.3	858.3

1. Excluding VAT.
Source: Österreichisches Statistisches Zentralamt, and Österreichisches Institut für Wirtschaftsforschung (WIFO).

Table B. **General government income and expenditure**

Sch billion

	1991	1992	1993	1994	1995	1996	1997	1998
Direct taxes	267.1	296.9	312.7	299.2	327.7	363.8	387.5	396.3
Household direct taxes	227.5	249.9	267.9	265.8	286.5	306.1	327.0	333.3
Corporate direct taxes	39.7	47.1	44.8	33.4	41.2	57.7	60.5	63.0
Indirect taxes	305.8	325.8	340.0	356.6	341.4	360.2	381.8	399.6
Social security contributions	238.9	262.3	280.0	300.5	315.8	327.8	332.7	342.5
Unfunded employee welfare contributions imputed	49.8	53.1	56.3	54.4	55.6	53.5	53.9	54.5
Compulsory fees, fines and penalties	5.5	5.5	6.0	6.5	6.4	6.8	7.1	7.4
Current transfers n.e.c. received from the rest of the world	0.9	0.7	0.7	0.8	9.2	5.2	5.5	5.5
Operating surplus and property income receivable	40.6	49.8	45.5	46.1	50.7	41.8	40.0	30.0
Current receipts	908.6	994.2	1 041.1	1 064.1	1 106.8	1 159.1	1 208.5	1 235.8
Final consumption expenditure [1]	348.3	375.2	405.0	425.9	440.4	446.4	463.0	472.5
Property income payable	81.9	87.5	91.9	91.1	102.4	106.8	101.0	105.2
Net casualty insurance premiums payable	0.4	0.4	0.4	0.4	0.4	0.5	0.4	0.4
Subsidies	61.5	64.0	68.8	58.2	63.1	64.8	64.0	62.0
Social security benefits and social assistance grants	199.9	212.5	229.6	247.3	262.2	274.1	284.0	304.0
Current transfers to private non-profit institutions serving household	103.7	117.1	142.3	150.7	148.8	148.8	148.4	143.0
Unfunded employee welfare benefits	80.8	85.9	91.5	96.0	100.5	103.3	104.5	111.0
Current transfers n.e.c. paid to the rest of the world	6.5	8.0	8.5	9.4	15.3	18.3	21.6	22.8
Current disbursements	883.0	950.6	1 038.1	1 079.1	1 133.1	1 163.0	1 186.9	1 220.9
Saving	25.7	43.6	3.1	−15.0	−26.3	−3.9	21.6	14.9
Consumption of fixed capital	13.5	13.8	14.5	15.1	15.7	16.2	16.8	17.3
Capital transfers received net, from:	−34.1	−30.4	−38.4	−36.6	−44.7	−40.6	−37.4	−36.5
Other resident sectors	−26.3	−26.9	−34.6	−33.9	−41.1	−37.2	−33.4	−33.2
The rest of the world	−1.0	−1.2	−1.2	−1.2	−0.7	−0.9	−0.9	−0.9
The public sector [2]	−6.8	−2.3	−2.6	−1.5	−2.9	−2.5	−3.1	−2.4
Finance of gross accumulation	5.1	27.0	−20.9	−36.5	−55.3	−28.3	1.0	−4.3
Gross capital formation	63.0	67.7	67.5	70.5	68.1	66.9	69.0	67.0
Purchases of land, net	0.5	0.0	1.2	2.5	−4.0	0.1	1.0	1.0
Net lending	−58.6	−40.7	−89.4	−109.3	−119.2	−95.7	−69.0	−72.3

Note: Data refer to the Bundesfinanzgesetz 1998 and may differ from the more updated data shown in the text of the Survey.
1.   Data differ from Table A due to a major revision of national accounts to Austria.
2.   Including net current transfers from public sector.
Source: Bundesministerium für Finanzen.

Table C. **Output, employment and productivity in industry**

	1990	1991	1992	1993	1994	1995	1996	1997	1998
Output in industry, 1990 = 100									
Total industry	100.0	101.9	100.7	99.2	103.2	108.3	109.1	115.3	119.2
Investment goods	100.0	105.3	102.6	97.8	101.0	109.5	110.2	116.3	122.8
Consumer goods	100.0	102.2	100.1	99.0	100.7	100.1	101.4	102.4	100.5
Intermediate goods	100.0	100.5	100.4	97.9	104.7	111.1	112.8	122.4	..
Manufacturing goods	100.0	101.7	100.9	98.1	103.3	107.7	110.1	..	..
Employment, thousands[1]	544.8	538.9	520.5	487.4	470.1	465.7	..	..	..
Monthly hours worked[2]	139	138	138	138	140	139	..	..	..
Wages and productivity									
Gross hourly earnings for wage earners (Sch)	120.7	127.9	135.3	142.0	147.4	153.9	159.8	162.7	166.2
Gross monthly earnings, employees (Sch)	25 143	26 593	28 208	29 613	30 791	32 193	33 397	34 160	35 036
Output per employee (1990 = 100)	100.0	102.4	101.3	98.4	102.1	108.3	..	..	..

1. Including administrative personnel.
2. Mining and manufacturing
Source: Österreichisches Institut für Wirtschaftsforschung, and Österreichisches Statistiches Zentralamt.

Table D. **Retail sales and prices**

(1990 = 100)

	1990	1991	1992	1993	1994	1995	1996	1997	1998
Retail sales	100.0	107.5	111.6	112.0	115.5	115.1	117.4	117.3	120.3
of which: durable	100.0	108.0	112.5	112.0	115.2	116.9	122.2	120.4	124.0
Prices									
Consumer prices									
Total	100.0	103.3	107.5	111.4	114.7	117.3	119.0	120.6	121.7
Food	100.0	104.1	108.2	111.3	113.4	112.8	113.4	115.3	117.4
Rent	100.0	104.8	111.0	117.4	124.9	134.4	142.5	148.1	152.7
Other goods and services	100.0	102.9	106.9	110.8	114.2	117.3	119.5	117.3	119.5
Wholesale prices									
Total	100.0	100.9	100.6	100.2	101.5	101.9	101.9	102.2	101.7
Agricultural goods	100.0	101.6	91.3	88.7	91.3	85.3	76.1	74.3	74.7
Food	100.0	102.6	107.8	108.8	109.9	103.0	104.4	104.9	106.8
Cost of construction									
(residential)	100.0	105.9	110.7	114.2	117.6	120.3	122.1	123.7	125.1

Source: Österreichisches Statistisches Zentralamt, and Österreichisches Institut für Wirtschaftsforschung.

Table E. **Money and banking**[1]
End of period
Sch billion

	1990	1991	1992	1993	1994	1995	1996	1997	1998
Interest rates (per cent)									
Discount rate	6.50	8.00	8.00	5.25	4.50	3.00	2.50	2.50	2.50
Average bond yield[2]	8.72	8.69	8.39	6.74	6.69	6.51	5.33	4.84	4.40
Money circulation and external reserves									
Notes and coins in circulation	124.7	133.4	141.2	149.8	158.3	168.6	176.7	178.8	176.7
Sight liabilities of the Central Bank	44.3	38.8	48.9	55.6	56.3	43.9	50.5	47.9	55.2
Gross external reserves of the Central Bank	130.3	140.1	167.4	202.4	208.3	201.6	219.0	210.0	281.4
of which: Gold	38.1	37.4	37.2	34.7	34.2	22.3	19.7	14.7	32.7
Credit institutions									
Credits to domestic non-banks	1 846.2	1 994.2	2 129.7	2 202.1	2 316.9	2 477.5	2 566.0	2 658.2	2 756.1
Deposits from domestic non-banks	1 503.8	1 613.9	1 680.3	1 751.9	1 850.8	1 941.6	1 985.4	2 024.8	2 146.5
Sight	155.9	170.8	180.9	207.2	222.0	266.4	284.5	306.1	350.1
Time[3]	185.8	172.4	136.9	118.0	131.4	123.6	116.8	100.9	148.8
Savings	1 162.1	1 270.7	1 362.5	1 426.7	1 497.4	1 551.6	1 584.2	1 617.8	1 647.7
Holdings of domestic Treasury bills	53.7	60.4	56.3	67.0	72.6	49.2	40.9	45.6	32.8
Holdings of other domestic securities	356.1	365.0	342.4	376.2	445.7	498.9	557.1	576.9	620.5
Foreign assets	843.9	846.8	915.9	1 012.4	1 039.5	1 138.5	1 254.6	1 450.2	1 523.8
Foreign liabilities	937.8	962.0	1 048.8	1 088.3	1 114.1	1 189.5	1 379.6	1 649.3	1 746.7

1. Totals may not add due to rounding.
2. Average effective yields on circulating issues.
3. Including funded borrowing of banks.
Source: Oesterreichische Nationalbank.

Table F. **The Federal budget**
National accounts basis
Sch billion

		Outcome						
	1991	1992	1993	1994	1995	1996	1997	1998
1. Current revenue	474.8	520.4	539.7	546.1	580.6	608.6	638.0	646.1
Direct taxes								
of households	154.7	169.1	181.8	185.2	207.7	215.0	233.4	245.7
Indirect taxes	213.2	229.0	236.9	245.1	229.9	243.5	265.1	281.0
Corporate taxes	29.8	36.4	34.3	25.9	33.5	50.0	52.5	44.0
Income from property								
and entrepreneurship	29.0	33.4	29.9	31.9	36.6	29.4	27.0	16.4
Current transfers from								
abroad	0.4	0.2	0.2	0.3	8.9	4.8	5.0	5.0
Other	47.7	52.3	56.6	57.7	64.0	65.9	55.0	54.0
2. Current expenditure	495.1	525.5	584.8	599.0	633.6	656.0	658.2	664.4
Goods and services	124.1	131.0	140.7	148.1	153.8	154.2	155.0	156.0
Subsidies	48.0	49.5	54.2	41.9	47.3	48.5	47.5	46.0
Property income payable	72.8	78.3	82.8	82.1	91.8	95.4	90.0	92.7
Transfers to abroad	2.0	2.1	2.7	3.5	8.7	11.5	14.7	15.4
Transfers to public								
authorities	121.4	125.4	140.0	151.3	159.8	173.4	178.3	188.0
Transfers to private								
households	77.8	87.2	108.6	113.2	110.2	108.8	106.7	98.3
Other	49.0	52.0	55.8	58.9	62.0	64.2	66.0	68.0
3. Net public savings (1-2)	−20.3	−5.1	−45.1	−52.9	−53.0	−47.4	−20.2	−18.3
4. Depreciation	3.1	3.1	3.3	3.4	3.6	3.7	3.8	3.9
5. Gross savings (3+4)	−17.2	−2.0	−41.8	−49.5	−49.4	−43.7	−16.4	−14.4
6. Gross asset formation	16.8	15.1	15.7	16.3	14.7	13.3	11.5	11.4
7. Balance of income-effective transactions (5-6)	−34.0	−17.1	−57.5	−65.8	−64.1	−57.0	−27.9	−25.8
8. Capital transfers (net)	39.3	41.2	43.8	43.3	51.2	50.1	46.6	47.5
9. Financial balance (7-8)	−73.3	−58.4	−101.4	−109.0	−115.3	−107.1	−73.5	−73.4

Note: Data refer to the Bundesfinanzgesetz 1998 and may differ from the more updated data shown in the text of the
Survey.
Source: Bundesministerium für Finanzen.

Table G. **Balance of payments**

Sch billion

	1992	1993	1994	1995	1996	1997	1998
Goods and services	18.7	12.5	−6.2	−20.6	−28.9	−39.2	−17.3
Merchandise	−84.1	−75.3	−90.2	−67.1	−77.0	−52.0	−50.8
Exports	488.8	468.4	513.8	581.4	613.9	716.1	772.0
Imports	572.9	543.7	604.0	648.5	690.9	768.0	822.8
Services, net	102.8	87.8	84.0	46.5	48.2	12.7	33.5
Of which: Travel	64.3	58.1	39.5	26.5	18.6	10.8	20.7
Exports	151.0	148.5	139.9	136.0	135.3	134.1	139.2
Imports	86.7	90.4	100.4	109.5	116.7	123.2	118.5
Investment income, net	−15.6	−12.4	−14.6	−16.2	−3.1	−1.4	−13.1
Transfers, net	−11.1	−11.7	−12.3	−17.3	−18.8	−20.7	−24.0
Official	−6.7	−7.8	−8.3	−14.3	−15.5	−18.8	−18.6
Private	−4.3	−3.9	−4.0	−3.0	−3.3	−1.9	−5.4
Current account	−8.0	−11.7	−33.1	−54.0	−50.8	−61.4	−54.5
Balance of capital transfers and financial transactions	−2.6	15.1	35.8	58.9	44.7	55.2	53.1
Of which: Balance of financial transactions:	−2.1	20.3	36.8	59.5	43.8	54.9	55.1
Direct investment	−2.9	−0.6	9.7	7.8	26.4	5.3	35.9
Austrian abroad	18.7	13.8	14.4	11.4	20.5	23.8	37.3
Foreign in Austria	15.7	13.2	24.0	19.2	46.9	29.1	73.2
Portfolio investment in shares and investment certificates	−0.1	6.6	4.1	5.7	18.2	2.4	−60.8
Austrian abroad	1.8	7.3	11.0	6.8	10.0	32.4	72.2
Foreign in Austria	1.7	13.8	15.0	12.5	28.2	34.8	11.4
Portfolio investment in fixed-interest securities	70.5	63.8	−6.9	88.4	−44.9	11.5	111.9
Foreign securities in Austria	27.9	14.9	41.5	23.0	75.8	91.1	80.2
Domestic securities	98.4	78.7	34.6	111.4	30.9	102.6	192.1
Other investors	−41.8	−22.9	40.6	−28.6	55.3	−0.3	8.2
Claims on foreigners	80.3	59.1	31.8	102.0	−9.0	63.3	22.1
Claims on domestic resident	38.5	36.2	72.4	73.4	46.4	63.1	30.4
Changes in official reserves	−27.8	−26.5	−10.6	−13.8	−11.1	35.9	−40.1
Errors and omissions	10.6	−3.4	−2.7	−4.9	6.1	6.2	1.3

Source: Oesterreichische Nationalbank.

Table H. **Merchandise trade by area**

Sch billion

	Imports					Exports				
	1993	1994	1995	1996	1997	1993	1994	1995	1996	1997
Total	563.6	629.8	657.3	712.6	789.6	466.3	512.5	575.8	611.9	714.2
OECD countries	499.09	554.2	585.9	632.2	695.5	405.02	444.4	497.2	527.3	608.8
OECD Europe	442.69	490.7	534.7	575.0	627.1	374.39	409.0	461.8	486.0	559.9
EU countries	390.34	430.2	473.6	504.7	544.8	305.53	331.9	376.8	392.7	443.7
Germany	234.07	252.3	290.3	305.5	329.0	182.18	195.5	219.2	229.0	250.7
Italy	50.86	55.7	58.1	62.7	66.8	36.89	41.7	51.1	50.9	59.3
France	24.79	29.7	31.6	34.2	37.0	20.71	23.3	25.5	26.2	29.5
United Kingdom	15.41	18.3	18.4	21.5	24.1	15.25	16.2	19.1	21.6	29.6
Switzerland	23.06	25.7	24.4	24.9	26.3	28.79	32.6	31.6	30.3	34.8
Other OECD	56.4	63.5	51.1	57.2	68.3	15.3	16.3	19.1	16.3	19.1
United States	24.81	27.5	28.1	31.8	42.2	15.39	17.9	17.2	19.5	26.1
Japan	24.80	27.0	16.4	17.2	17.3	7.16	8.0	7.6	9.4	9.0
Non-OECD countries	64.49	75.6	71.4	80.4	94.1	61.29	68.1	78.6	84.5	105.3
CIS	8.73	11.9	13.1	13.7	15.2	7.62	9.1	10.8	11.3	14.1
Africa	11.33	10.4	9.7	12.5	14.0	6.43	7.9	6.8	6.3	7.2
Latin America	3.20	4.3	3.3	3.0	3.8	2.96	3.6	4.8	5.5	7.5
Middle East	4.84	5.4	4.0	4.4	5.8	9.44	8.5	8.3	8.8	10.3
Far East	25.52	30.0	24.4	26.8	30.8	16.57	16.9	19.6	20.1	21.3

Source: OECD, *Monthly Statistics of Foreign Trade, Series A.*

Table I. **Labour-market indicators**

	Preceding 1987 Peak	Trough	1990	1992	1994	1995	1996	1997	1998
Evolution									
Unemployment rate (surveys)									
Total	1983 = 4.1	1973 = 1.1	3.1	3.5	4.2	3.9	4.3	4.4	4.4
Male	1984 = 3.9	1973 = 0.7	2.8	3.4	3.3	3.3	4.1	4.1	..
Women	1983 = 5.1	1973 = 1.7	3.6	3.7	4.0	4.5	4.7	4.9	..
Unemployment rate (registered)									
Total	1987 = 5.6	1974 = 1.5	5.4	6.0	6.5	6.6	7.0	7.1	7.2
Male	1987 = 5.5	1973 = 0.6	4.9	5.7	6.4	6.4	6.9	6.9	6.9
Women	1987 = 5.7	1980 = 2.3	6.0	6.2	6.7	6.8	7.3	7.4	7.5
Youth			2.6	2.5	2.8	2.9	3.3	..	..
Share of long-term unemployment [1]			15.8	20.9	22.8	27.5	25.6	28.7	..
Productivity index, 1991 = 100			98.5	99.9	102.9	105.0	107.9	110.3	113.2
Monthly hours of work in industry (wage earners) billions of hours			139	138	140	139	..	..	..
Structural or institutional characteristics									
Participation rates [2]									
Global			67.7	69.4	71.6	72.1	71.3	71.4	..
Male			80.1	80.7	81.0	81.6	80.9	80.8	..
Women			55.4	58.0	62.1	62.3	61.5	61.9	..
Employment/population between 16 and 64 years [1]			65.5	66.9	69.2	69.2	68.4	68.4	..
Employment by sector									
Agriculture – per cent of total			7.9	7.1	7.2	7.4	7.3	6.7	..
– per cent change			1.2	–2.4	7.7	3.3	–3.2	–7.1	..
Industry – per cent of total			36.8	35.6	33.2	32.0	31.0	30.1	..
– per cent change			1.6	–1.7	–4.3	–2.9	–4.4	–2.8	..
Services – per cent of total			55.3	57.4	59.6	60.6	61.8	63.2	..
– per cent change			2.5	5.1	8.1	2.2	0.6	2.6	..
Part-time work [1]			9.9	10.0	12.1	10.6	10.7	10.8	..
Non-filled vacancies, per cent of dependent employment			1.8	1.4	0.9	0.8	0.6	0.6	0.7
Social insurance as a per cent of compensation			18.1	18.3	18.6	18.4	18.4	19.9	20.1

1. From 1995 based on the European Labour Force survey.
2. Total labour force (including self employment)/population 15 to 64 years, OECD Labour Force Statistics.
Source: Statistical Yearbook; WIFO; OECD estimates; OECD, Labour Force Statistics; OECD, Employment Outlook.

Table J. **Public sector**

	1970	1980	1990	1995	1998
A. Budget indicators: General government accounts, % of GDP					
Current receipts	38.8	45.4	46.2	47.5	47.3
Non-interest expenditure	36.6	44.7	44.6	48.2	45.3
Primary budget balance	1.8	0.0	0.8	−1.5	1.5
Gross interest	0.6	1.7	3.2	3.6	3.7
General government budget balance	1.2	−1.7	−2.4	−5.1	−2.1
Of which: Federal government	0.2	−2.6	−3.3	−5.0	−2.8
B. The structure of expenditure, % of GDP					
Government expenditure					
Transfers [1]	15.1	18.9	20.0	22.6	21.7
Subsidies	1.7	2.9	2.8	2.6	2.3
General expenditure	14.3	17.6	17.6	18.9	18.3
Education	2.9	3.8	3.9	4.3	..
Health	3.2	4.3	4.6	5.2	..
Social security and welfare	2.6	3.2	3.2	3.4	..

	Prior to Tax Reform of 1988	Under the Tax Reform of 1988
C. Tax rates		
Personal income tax		
Top rate	62	50
Lower rate	21	10
Average tax rate	12.7	11.5
Social security tax rate [2]		
Blue-collar workers	38.6	38.6
White-collar workers	34.5	34.5
Basic VAT rate	20	20
Corporation tax rate		
Top rate	55	30
Lower rate	30	30

1.   Social secutity payments and other transfers payments.
2.   The sum of employees' and employers' contributions to health, accident, pension and unemployment insurance.
Source: OECD, National Accounts; Ministry of Finance.

Table K. **Production structure and performance indicators**

A. Production structure (1983 prices)

	GDP share (per cent of total industry GDP)					Employment share (per cent of total employment in industry)				
	1980	1990	1994	1995	1996	1980	1990	1994	1995	1996
Tradeables										
Agriculture	4.4	3.9	3.4	3.2	3.2	1.9	1.4	1.3	1.3	1.3
Mining and quarrying	2.2	0.9	0.7	0.7	0.7	0.9	0.5	0.4	0.4	0.4
Manufacturing	29.1	29.2	28.0	27.5	27.3	38.7	33.9	30.1	29.9	29.3
Non-tradeables										
Electricity	3.9	3.8	3.9	3.8	3.8	1.7	1.7	1.6	1.6	1.6
Construction	9.4	7.5	8.4	8.1	8.2	12.1	11.0	12.8	12.9	12.9
Wholesale and retail trade, restaurants and hotels	22.3	23.0	22.3	22.8	22.5	23.5	26.1	27.1	27.1	27.3
Transport, storage and communication	7.4	8.0	8.8	8.9	9.1	9.4	9.8	9.7	9.5	9.5
Finance, insurance, real estate and business services	17.1	19.3	20.3	20.7	20.9	8.3	10.5	11.2	11.5	11.7
Community, social and personal services	4.1	4.2	4.3	4.3	4.4	3.6	5.2	5.9	6.0	6.1

B. Industrial sector performance

	Productivity growth (sector GDP/sector employment)					Investment share, current prices (per cent of total)				
	1980	1990	1994	1995	1996	1980	1990	1994	1995	1996
Tradeables										
Agriculture	9.0	4.1	8.5	-3.5	2.0	6.8	5.2	4.1	..	..
Mining and quarrying	7.3	2.7	3.0	4.1	-2.5	1.1	0.5	0.5	..	..
Manufacturing	4.1	3.2	6.4	1.8	4.4	18.9	19.3	13.7	..	..
Non-tradeables										
Electricity	4.0	5.7	1.4	4.2	0.1	6.8	5.3	4.8	..	..
Construction	-1.5	2.4	4.7	-0.5	3.9	4.8	4.0	3.9	..	..
Wholesale and retail trade, restaurants and hotels	-3.8	2.5	0.3	5.1	1.0	11.5	12.0	12.1	..	..
Transport, storage and communication	6.5	4.9	6.3	7.3	5.7	13.6	14.3	13.4	..	..
Finance, insurance, real estate and business services	3.3	-0.1	-3.3	2.2	2.1	33.5	35.7	43.4	..	..
Community, social and personal services	0.1	0.2	-2.1	1.2	3.0	3.1	3.6	4.1	..	..

Table K. **Production structure and performance indicators** (cont.)

	Numbers of entreprises (per cent of total)					Numbers of employees (per cent of total)				
	1971	1980	1989	1990	1991	1971	1980	1989	1990	1991
C. Other indicators										
Enterprises ranged by size of employees										
1 to 4	..	18.3	40.4	38.4	37.7	..	0.3	0.7	0.7	0.7
5 to 49	57.9	49.0	37.7	38.6	38.8	11.2	11.2	12.4	12.2	12.4
50 to 499	38.3	29.6	20.0	20.9	21.5	48.6	46.6	48.9	49.8	51.6
more than 500	3.9	3.1	2.0	2.1	2.0	40.2	41.9	38.0	37.3	35.4
	1987	1988	1989	1990	1991	1992	1993	1994	1995	1996
R&D as percentage of manufacturing output	6.21	6.47	6.73	7.17	7.81	8.23	8.81	9.33	9.60	9.68

Source: OECD, National Accounts; Österreichisches Statistisches Handbuch.

BASIC STATISTICS:

INTERNATIONAL COMPARISONS

	Units	Reference period [1]	Australia	Austria
Population				
Total	Thousands	1997	18 532	8 072
Inhabitants per sq. km	Number	1997	2	96
Net average annual increase over previous 10 years	%	1997	1.3	0.6
Employment				
Total civilian employment (TCE)[2]	Thousands	1997	8 430	3 685
of which:				
Agriculture	% of TCE	1997	5.2	6.8
Industry	% of TCE	1997	22.1	30.3
Services	% of TCE	1997	72.7	63.8
Gross domestic product (GDP)				
At current prices and current exchange rates	Bill. US$	1997	392.9	206.2
Per capita	US$	1997	21 202	25 549
At current prices using current PPPs[3]	Bill. US$	1997	406.8	186.3
Per capita	US$	1997	21 949	23 077
Average annual volume growth over previous 5 years	%	1997	4.1	1.9
Gross fixed capital formation (GFCF)	% of GDP	1997	21.5	24.1
of which:				
Machinery and equipment	% of GDP	1997	10.3 (96)	8.8 (96)
Residential construction	% of GDP	1997	4.4 (96)	6.2 (96)
Average annual volume growth over previous 5 years	%	1997	7.3	2.8
Gross saving ratio[4]	% of GDP	1997	18.4	23
General government				
Current expenditure on goods and services	% of GDP	1997	16.7	19.4
Current disbursements[5]	% of GDP	1996	34.8	48
Current receipts	% of GDP	1996	35.4	47.9
Net official development assistance	% of GNP	1996	0.28	0.24
Indicators of living standards				
Private consumption per capita using current PPP's[3]	US$	1997	13 585	12 951
Passenger cars, per 1 000 inhabitants	Number	1995	477	447
Telephones, per 1 000 inhabitants	Number	1995	510	465
Television sets, per 1 000 inhabitants	Number	1994	489	480
Doctors, per 1 000 inhabitants	Number	1996	2.5	2.8
Infant mortality per 1 000 live births	Number	1996	5.8	5.1
Wages and prices (average annual increase over previous 5 years)				
Wages (earnings or rates according to availability)	%	1998	1.5	5.2
Consumer prices	%	1998	2.0	1.8
Foreign trade				
Exports of goods, fob*	Mill. US$	1998	55 882	61 754
As % of GDP	%	1997	15.6	28.4
Average annual increase over previous 5 years	%	1998	5.6	9
Imports of goods, cif*	Mill. US$	1998	60 821	68 014
As % of GDP	%	1997	15.3	31.4
Average annual increase over previous 5 years	%	1998	7.5	7
Total official reserves[6]	Mill. SDR's	1998	10 942	14 628 (97)
As ratio of average monthly imports of goods	Ratio	1998	2.2	2.7 (97)

* At current prices and exchange rates.
1. Unless otherwise stated.
2. According to the definitions used in OECD Labour Force Statistics.
3. PPPs = Purchasing Power Parities.
4. Gross saving = Gross national disposable income minus private and government consumption.

EMPLOYMENT OPPORTUNITIES

Economics Department, OECD

The Economics Department of the OECD offers challenging and rewarding opportunities to economists interested in applied policy analysis in an international environment. The Department's concerns extend across the entire field of economic policy analysis, both macro-economic and microeconomic. Its main task is to provide, for discussion by committees of senior officials from Member countries, documents and papers dealing with current policy concerns. Within this programme of work, three major responsibilities are:

- to prepare regular surveys of the economies of individual Member countries;
- to issue full twice-yearly reviews of the economic situation and prospects of the OECD countries in the context of world economic trends;
- to analyse specific policy issues in a medium-term context for the OECD as a whole, and to a lesser extent for the non-OECD countries.

The documents prepared for these purposes, together with much of the Department's other economic work, appear in published form in the *OECD Economic Outlook, OECD Economic Surveys, OECD Economic Studies* and the Department's *Working Papers* series.

The Department maintains a world econometric model, INTERLINK, which plays an important role in the preparation of the policy analyses and twice-yearly projections. The availability of extensive cross-country data bases and good computer resources facilitates comparative empirical analysis, much of which is incorporated into the model.

The Department is made up of about 80 professional economists from a variety of backgrounds and Member countries. Most projects are carried out by small teams and last from four to eighteen months. Within the Department, ideas and points of view are widely discussed; there is a lively professional interchange, and all professional staff have the opportunity to contribute actively to the programme of work.

Skills the Economics Department is looking for:

a) Solid competence in using the tools of both microeconomic and macroeconomic theory to answer policy questions. Experience indicates that this normally requires the equivalent of a Ph.D. in economics or substantial relevant professional experience to compensate for a lower degree.

b) Solid knowledge of economic statistics and quantitative methods; this includes how to identify data, estimate structural relationships, apply basic techniques of time series analysis, and test hypotheses. It is essential to be able to interpret results sensibly in an economic policy context.

c) A keen interest in and extensive knowledge of policy issues, economic developments and their political/social contexts.

d) Interest and experience in analysing questions posed by policy-makers and presenting the results to them effectively and judiciously. Thus, work experience in government agencies or policy research institutions is an advantage.

e) The ability to write clearly, effectively, and to the point. The OECD is a bilingual organisation with French and English as the official languages. Candidates must have excellent knowledge of one of these languages, and some knowledge of the other. Knowledge of other languages might also be an advantage for certain posts.

f) For some posts, expertise in a particular area may be important, but a successful candidate is expected to be able to work on a broader range of topics relevant to the work of the Department. Thus, except in rare cases, the Department does not recruit narrow specialists.

g) The Department works on a tight time schedule with strict deadlines. Moreover, much of the work in the Department is carried out in small groups. Thus, the ability to work with other economists from a variety of cultural and professional backgrounds, to supervise junior staff, and to produce work on time is important.

General information

The salary for recruits depends on educational and professional background. Positions carry a basic salary from FF 318 660 or FF 393 192 for Administrators (economists) and from FF 456 924 for Principal Administrators (senior economists). This may be supplemented by expatriation and/or family allowances, depending on nationality, residence and family situation. Initial appointments are for a fixed term of two to three years.

Vacancies are open to candidates from OECD Member countries. The Organisation seeks to maintain an appropriate balance between female and male staff and among nationals from Member countries.

For further information on employment opportunities in the Economics Department, contact:

Management Support Unit
Economics Department
OECD
2, rue André-Pascal
75775 PARIS CEDEX 16
FRANCE

E-Mail: eco.contact@oecd.org

Applications citing ''ECSUR'', together with a detailed *curriculum vitae* in English or French, should be sent to the Head of Personnel at the above address.

The Electronic Advantage
Ask for our
free Catalogue

The Fast and Easy way to work with statistics and graphs!

- Cut and paste capabilities
- Quick search & find functions
- Zoom for magnifying graphics
- Uses ACROBAT software
  (included free of charge)
- Works on Windows

OECD on the WEB: **www.oecd.org**

-->%

Please **FAX** or **MAIL** this page to the OECD Paris,
———— or to one of the four OECD Centres (*see overleaf*) ————

Where to send your request:

In Austria, Germany and Switzerland

OECD CENTRE BONN
August-Bebel-Allee 6,
D-53175 Bonn
Tel.: (49-228) 959 1215
Fax: (49-228) 959 1218
E-mail: bonn.contact@oecd.org
Internet: www.oecd.org/bonn

In Latin America

OECD CENTRE MEXICO
Edificio INFOTEC
Av. San Fernando No. 37
Col. Toriello Guerra
Tlalpan C.P. 14050,
Mexico D.F.
Tel.: (52-5) 528 10 38
Fax: (52-5) 606 13 07
E-mail: mexico.contact@oecd.org
Internet: rtn.net.mx/ocde/

In the United States

OECD CENTER WASHINGTON
2001 L Street N.W., Suite 650
Washington, DC 20036-4922
Tel.: (202) 785 6323
Toll free: (1 800) 456-6323
Fax: (202) 785 0350
E-mail: washington.contact@oecd.org
Internet: www.oecdwash.org

In Asia

OECD CENTRE TOKYO
Landic Akasaka Bldg.
2-3-4 Akasaka, Minato-ku,
Tokyo 107-0052
Tel.: (81-3) 3586 2016
Fax: (81-3) 3584 7929
E-mail : center@oecdtokyo.org
Internet: www.oecdtokyo.org

In the rest of the world

OECD PARIS CENTRE
2 rue André-Pascal, 75775 Paris Cedex 16, France
Fax: 33 (0)1 49 10 42 76 **Tel:** 33 (0)1 49 10 42 35
E-mail : sales@oecd.org
Internet : www.oecd.org
ONLINE ORDERS: www.oecd.org/publications (secure payment with credit card)

OECD PUBLICATIONS, 2, rue André-Pascal, 75775 PARIS CEDEX 16
PRINTED IN FRANCE
(10 1999 11 1 P) ISBN 92-64-16984-9 – No. 50635 1999
ISSN 0376-6438